# THE KETTERING ALBUM

Grant of Arms by the Earl Marshal and Hereditary Marshal of
England, dated 26 September 1938.

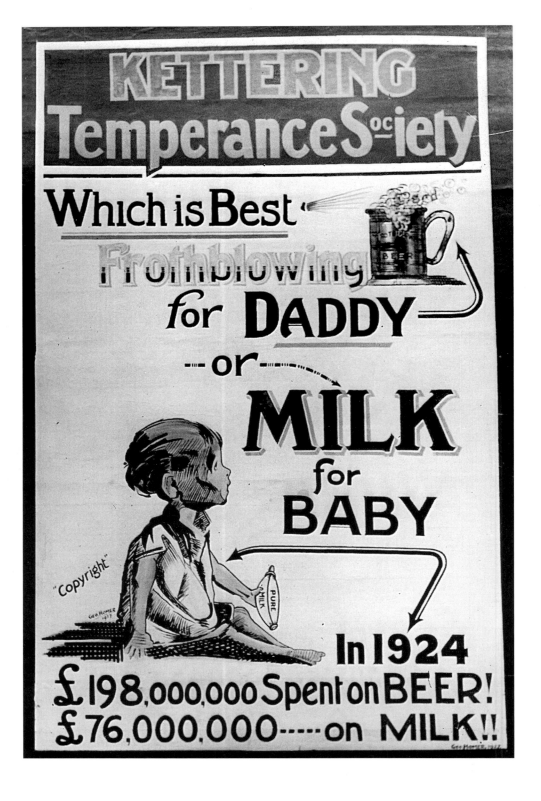

# THE KETTERING ALBUM

## More Pictures from the Past

Tony Smith

W. D. WHARTON

WELLINGBOROUGH

The author dedicates this book
to the memory of his friend and
former *Evening Telegraph* colleague
Ken Hankins, who died on 12 October 1996

First published in 1997 by
W. D. Wharton
37 Sheep Street
Wellingborough
Northamptonshire NN8 1BX

Text copyright © Tony Smith 1997

Tony Smith asserts his moral right
to be identified as the author of this work

ISBN 1 899597 05  0

End-paper captions:
Front left: Bird's-eye view of Kettering in the 1950s.
(*Kettering Civic Society*)
Front right: Kettering Market Place in 1898. (*Tony Smith*)

Rear left: Aerial picture of Wicksteed Park in the 1920s.
(*Kettering Civic Society*)
Rear right: Feast Sunday parade, Dalkeith Place on 4 July 1926.
(*Tony Smith*)

Designed and typeset by John Hardaker, Wollaston, Northants
Pictures scanned by Slade Graphics, Kettering, Northants
Printed and bound in Great Britain by
Stanley L. Hunt (Printers) Ltd, Midland Road, Rushden, Northants

*Parish Church, Kettering.*

# Contents

# Acknowledgements

My heartfelt thanks go to the following for the use of photographs: Kettering Civic Society, Robert Wharton, Dick Fairey, Fuller Baptist Church, Jack Cross, Leo Corvesor, Winnie Bailey, Kettering Fire Station, Brian Hughes, John Darker, Timsons, St Peter's School, Park Junior School, Ronald Tree Nursery, Reg Abbott, Brian Old, Pam Dyson, Robert Wicksteed and Tony Ireson.

Others who gave invaluable help were: Malcolm Robinson at Kettering Reference Library, Catherine Nisbet at Kettering Manor House Museum, Northamptonshire Record Office, Carmel Crawley at the *Evening Telegraph*, Jim Worthington, Bill Lewin, Obed Bye, Bob Bright, John Pemble, Jane Watson, Fred Nursey and the late Simon Thornton. Special thanks to Arthur Heath for the foreword.

Main text sources include:

*Kettering Leader and Guardian*
*Northamptonshire Evening Telegraph*
*Northampton Independent*
The Frank Thompson collection
*Kettering Temp George V, 1912*
*Old Kettering and its Defenders* by Tony Ireson
*Old Kettering – a View from the 1930s* (Vols. 1–4) by
    Tony Ireson
*Kettering British Industries, 1891*
*A Walk Around Kettering* by Kettering Civic Society
*A Pictorial History of Kettering* by The Rotary Club of
    Kettering Huxloe
*Souvenir of the Kettering Charter of Incorporation, 1938*
*Kelly's Directory of Northamptonshire* (various)
*An Illustrated History of United Counties* by Roger Warwick
*The Diamond Jubilee History of the Kettering Industrial
    Co-operative Society*
*Windmills of Northamptonshire* by Trevor Stainwright

Market Square.

NORTH SEA

IRISH SEA

Rushton Lodge.

KETTERING.

Silver St.

Bristol Channel

Sheep St.

Cranford Church and Hall.

ENGLISH CHANNEL
KETTERING, ENGLAND.

# Foreword

There will be, I am sure, countless readers of *The Kettering Album* who, like myself, will wish to congratulate Tony Smith on this, his second book of photographs showing Kettering and its citizens of days gone by.

Of course, *The Kettering Album* is far more than just a collection of old photographs, it is a valuable reference source for all ages and for generations of townspeople to come. To most of us, though, it will be the subject matter of each and every picture that will grip our interest and tug nostalgically at our memories.

Tony displays the practised hand of the professional journalist by his careful selection of photographs which, chapter by chapter, enable the reader to turn instantly to the pictures in which he or she has a particular interest.

Inevitably, I suppose, I flicked the pages immediately to 'Buildings' – a chapter dominated by a fine picture of the old Grammar School that once graced Gold Street (page 56). As Tony so poignantly describes – 'A crowd of disbelieving townsfolk gathered in Gold Street on the morning of Sunday 29 November 1964 as workers reduced the old Grammar School to rubble.' Alerted by a telephone call from Tony Ireson, I joined that group of shocked residents and watched helplessly as this once fine building (also featured in colour on the back cover) crashed to the ground.

Sadly, the old Grammar School was soon to be joined in crumbled masonry by the Post Office buildings in Gold Street and Beech House in Tanners Lane, which Kettering Civic Society battled in vain to save during the 1970s. These buildings have long since gone, but this fine book brings them faithfully back for all to see and to mourn their loss.

Transport enthusiasts will note in the picture of Brake's shop in Gold Street (page 36) a 1930s Morris 8, reminding me of an identical model that regularly took me, my wife, two children, dog and a fortnight's luggage to the East Coast. Another picture shows an open 'charabanc', a vehicle that demanded tough weather-hardened passengers indeed.

This is unashamedly a book of memories to some; a surprise to others; a delight to many. To most it is all of those things, for Tony shows Kettering as it really was – not a perfect town but one of a size that its people could cope with, a pleasant place to live and work in.

Like *Kettering Revisited*, I have found this sequel fascinating to read and to browse over time and time again, a tribute to the many laborious hours of research spent in its compilation. I'm sure that for years to come it will provide endless entertainment and irrefutable proof of what Kettering used to look like.

I therefore commend Tony Smith for providing us with such a delightful book, and feel certain it will be regarded as a 'definitive' work by local historians in the twenty-first century, just as F. W. Bull's *History of Kettering* was by scholars in 1891.

Arthur Heath MBE
Chairman Kettering Civic Society

# Kettering Revisited – An Update

Much has happened since my first book, *Kettering Revisited: Pictures from the Past*, was published over three years ago.

The opening of the A14 in July 1994 has brought new industry and commerce to the area. New housing estates have sprung up on the edge of town and, sometimes, in the most unlikely places in the town itself.

Kettering's new £13m Leisure Village closed and then opened again under new management. New pubs, hotels, restaurants and superstores have been built to cater for a fast expanding population.

There are exciting plans for a multi-screen cinema complex off Pytchley Road, while talks continue on the revamp of the town centre behind Dryland Street.

The march of progress inevitably means that more of our older buildings and businesses are vanishing. In 1996 alone the old Timpsons factory in Bath Road and the former Freeman, Hardy & Willis premises in Mill Road have made way for new development.

Country and equestrian footwear firm Allen and Caswell of Cornwall Road was sold by owner William Caswell after 99 years in the town.

But 1996 was also a year for reflecting on past achievements, with Wicksteed Park celebrating its 75th anniversary, printing press firm Timsons clocking up a century, and Fuller Church marking its 300th birthday.

Timsons celebrated its centenary in 1996.
This is its founder Arthur Timson (1871-1954)

And with the *Evening Telegraph* and Kettering General Hospital both celebrating centenaries this year, it seems an appropriate time to have another lingering look back at the town's history and past glories.

*Kettering Revisited* introduced readers to the main streets and long-gone buildings of yesteryear. This latest volume goes a step further with more in-depth research into local events of the day and the people connected with them.

*The Kettering Album* is more than just a collection of nostalgic pictures to flick through in an idle moment. It is hoped readers will pause to read the stories behind each photograph and learn how this ancient market town was shaped and changed – for good or bad – over many decades of development.

Compiling this book evoked personal childhood memories of buying pea-shooters from Bell and Billows and ammunition from Kettering Corn Stores; and of biking to Jack Cross the newsagents every Tuesday evening to get my comics before they went on sale elsewhere on Wednesday morning!

But I found it just as fascinating reading fading old newspaper reports of huge parades and carnivals, lavish Coronation festivities, respectful obituaries of leading townsmen, and official openings of grand old buildings – many of which, sadly, have since been demolished.

Fuller Baptist Church – founded 300 years ago.

Of course, this book would not have been possible without the generous loan of some tremendous old pictures from various sources, in particular Kettering Civic Society, which gave me access to its archives.

My gratitude to all those who so kindly shared their photographs and memories is expressed elsewhere. And who knows – if anyone out there has a dusty collection of old Kettering pictures in their attic, there may be a third volume for us all to enjoy one day …

Tony Smith
Kettering
1997

# 1. Victoriana

The top of Market Street at its junction with London Road in the early 1890s. At the rear is the town's first telephone exchange opened by the National Telephone Company in 1890. At first it was based here in a narrow passage off shop premises occupied by William Lee, a dealer in goods from London, Birmingham and Sheffield. His two daughters became the first operators. To begin with there were only six subscribers, but in 1895, when this number had grown to 27, a new exchange was opened next to the laundry in nearby Church Walk. The buildings in the picture were knocked down to make way for the National Infant School, with the teacher's house on the London Road corner. This was later occupied by the old Weights and Measures department, and the corner house is now an estate agent's office. The old exchange building was used by the Home Guard during World War II. (*Tony Smith*)

# VIEW OF "THE GEORGE HOTEL" SHEWING THE LONG FRONTAGE TO SHEEP STREET.

The George Hotel and posting house in Sheep Street in 1878. Built largely of red brick, it had an imposing appearance and a portico over the entrance opposite the Parish Church. Advertised as the nearest hotel to the station, its stables consisted of 10 loose boxes, a fire stall, a four-stall and two-stall stable, two coach houses, a house for eight cows and a large pig yard. At one time the landlords of the George and the White Hart (Royal) Hotel, Timothy Holland and Richard Stockburn, were both Parish Church wardens. The hotel was built on the site of the eighteenth century Cock Inn. Its frontage, pictured here, is now Piccadilly Buildings, built in 1926 (see page 45). (*Tony Smith*)

The Gold Street–Newland Street corner in 1898. In earlier times Newland pond was in the centre of the crossroads. The picture shows W. H. Baker's shop and other buildings awaiting demolition. Mr Baker, a furnisher, clothier, jeweller and pawnbroker, came to Kettering from Hull in 1896 and became president of Kettering Harriers and the Chamber of Trade, and an urban councillor. He was also an inventor who claimed to have created the white line for traffic control in 1884. (*Tony Smith*)

An 1860 picture of Benfords, the High Street tailors and drapers, next to the Royal Hotel. On the right is Mr J. H. Wheeler's jewellers and watchmakers shop. When he retired, Mr Wheeler had Ruby Cottage built in Ebenezer Place. Tired of doing nothing, he began selling jewellery from his front room before taking back his old shop with his nephew Mr J. G. Field, who inherited the business when Mr Wheeler died in 1888. (*Tony Smith*)

Goosey's, the undertakers and drapers in the High Street, pictured in the 1890s. The business was established by John Goosey, whose son William Gill Goosey, grandson Frank and his son Francis were all born on the premises. Their black horse-drawn hearses were a common sight, and they also hired out marquees for weddings, garden parties and sports events. The shop, house, outbuildings, stables, garden and orchard occupied the present site of the Gala Bingo Club, which began as the Regal Cinema in 1936 and later became the Granada. (*Tony Smith*)

The Elworthy family set up their brewery in 1871, its range of buildings crammed into a site between Gold Street, Tanners Lane and Lower Street. They brewed Kettering beer for three generations and sold it at the Crown Inn in Gold Street. John Elworthy, who took over the business from his father William in 1914, was president of the Poppies and clerk of the course for Kettering races. The brewery closed in 1931 and most of its buildings were knocked down to accommodate the Gold Street development in the 1970s, but its red brick malting tower is still a Lower Street landmark. (*Tony Smith*)

## A.R. Brake

A view of popular pawnbroker and jeweller A. R. Brake's impressive shop in Gold Street in 1896. Arthur Richard Brake came to Kettering in 1887 and established his store on the commanding corner of Gold Street and Meeting Lane, formerly Moore's Toyshop. In 1892 Mr Brake, born in Marston Trussell, near Market Harborough, added to his premises the building known as Jenkinson's block in Meeting Lane and began selling furniture, prams and pianos in a range of 16 showrooms. On the jewellery side, there were separate entrances for customers and persons plying goods, of course. In 1897 he added a branch in Montagu Street and three years later another on the corner of Regent Street and Wellington Street. The building is still a jewellers – H. Samuel (formerly Ratners). (*Kettering Civic Society*)

Percy Wallis's picture of Sheep Street in 1884 shows the Royal Iron Works on the site now occupied by the library and art gallery. The iron and brass foundry, making agricultural implements, was run by the inventor William Henry Smith and his son James. William was an active member of Toller Chapel and his inventions won many prizes at international exhibitions in London, Paris and Hamburg between 1855 and 1878. The Smiths lived at Stamford House in Headlands, which later became Hillside, the High School's junior department. After William's death, a Mr Weston took over for a while until the entire block, which included the Manor House and field, was bought by the local authority. The old stone wall continued up Bowling Green Road to the Cattle Market. (*Dick Fairey*)

## Hazelwood Lane

A Victorian picture of the two seventeenth century cottages in Hazelwood Lane (off West Street), named after a farmer who used to live there. The building nearest the camera became the birthplace of non-conformity in Kettering when protestant dissenters held their first services there in August 1662. Their absent pastor was former Kettering rector, the Rev. John Maidwell, one of 46 county clergymen to leave the established church, who was in hiding in Marston Trussell. These non-conformists set up the first Congregational church in Allen's Yard behind the present Midland Bank. In October 1956 the two derelict cottages were demolished. Although listed as being of special architectural and historical interest, they had become dangerous and beyond repair. Workmen were astonished at the nearly-new condition of the oak floorboards and stair treads, which had no trace of woodworm. (*Kettering Civic Society*)

## Gas Street

This pretty thatched cottage could be found in Gas Street (now Meadow Road) during the 1890s. On the right, selling Phipps ale (later Watneys) is the grocers and outdoor beerhouse belonging to Miss Jane Caroline Bell, a popular shop off Kettering town centre until the early 1930s. The site, on the corner of Trafalgar Road, is now occupied by the rear of Marks & Spencer, a pedestrianised area which includes a tree garden and a park bench. The road was originally called Goosepasture Lane, after a small common stocked with geese at the west end. It was renamed Gas Street after gasworks were built at the bottom of the road along Northfield Avenue. It has also been known anciently as Mill Lane, after a hemp mill on the aforementioned common, and even Meadow Lane. (*Kettering Civic Society*)

A picture of the same mill, minus sails, a few years later. By the 1860s both this an[d] the post mill in Weekley Road were operated by the Coleman family – William Coleman Sr. at the post mill and his son, William, at the tower. On 31 January 189[ ] was bought by the Kettering School Board which kept enough land to build a scho[ol] and sold the remainder for house building in 1894. (*Kettering Civic Society*)

This three-storey tower mill, pictured in 1890, could be found off Rockingham Road between Dryden Street and Buccleuch Street. It was built in 1821 to replace a post mill by Kettering carpenter William Cunnington. Made of stone encased in brick, it was later bought by Cunnington's niece, who sold it to Rothwell farmer William Chater, who ran it together with a bakery until his son, also William, took it over in 1858. (*Kettering Civic Society*)

The ruins of Kettering post mill at the turn of the century, showing the windshaft and its brake and tail wheels. It is believed to have been built in 1817 to succeed an earlier mill dating from 1609, and was once owned by Kettering banker Thomas Henry Gotch. One of the sails broke off in a violent storm but, after the opposite one was removed to restore the balance, it continued to operate for many years with just two sails. It eventually became unsafe and the half-dismantled ruin collapsed on 17 May 1900, the day Mafeking was relieved. The nearby millhouse survived until 1962, when it was knocked down for a housing estate. The post mill is still remembered in the shape of Windmill Avenue, Windmill Walk and Mill Dale Road. (*Kettering Civic Society*)

# 2. Streets and Town Centre

This picture of the dinner-hour rush at the Rockingham Road junction with Regent Street appeared in the *Kettering Leader and Guardian* in November 1925 under the headline 'A dangerous crossing'. On the right are some of the women employed at the Co-op clothing factory in Dryden Street. The paper reported: 'If there is no policeman on duty to direct the traffic, pedestrians, cyclists and motorists are to be seen dashing in all directions, and the wonder is that not more accidents have occurred at this spot.' On the day in question there was a constable on duty – a measure urged by the *Leader and Guardian* months before. (*Kettering Civic Society*)

The Carey Mission House in Lower Street in 1910. In the late eighteenth century it was the home of Martha Wallis, widow of wool dyer Beeby Wallis, and the Baptist Missionary Society was formed here in 1792 (see page 175). For many years this spectacular seven-bayed building was the home of industrialist J. T. Stockburn, who established a corset factory in Northall Street. The house was converted into flats for the elderly by the Baptist Housing Association in March 1974. The further 32 flats built in its grounds in 1979 were named Martha Wallis Court. On the left of the picture, in the distance, is the former Charles East shoe factory (later Walker Last), pulled down in March 1984 to make way for Windsor Gardens, more homes for retired people. The road junction is now controlled by traffic lights. (*Tony Smith*)

A rainy day in Newland Street during the 1930s. Pictured is the old Fleur de Lys, a popular seventeenth century pub nicknamed the 'Flue' by regulars. Together with the Vine and Hare and Hounds in nearby Rockingham Road, it was a favourite watering hole for Kettering furnacemen. Phipps closed it down in 1960, and the following year it was demolished to make way for a new £25,000 block of shops. On the right of the picture are the former Co-op central store and arcade, leading to Montagu Street. These were opened on 31 May 1930 by the wife of Health Minister Arthur Greenwood, who had hurt himself in a fall and couldn't perform the ceremony. (*Kettering Civic Society*)

On the opposite page: An overhead picture of Kettering High Street in the 1900s, taken from the chambers of the then London City and Midland Bank. These were built by the Leicestershire Banking Company in the early 1870s on a site previously occupied by ironmonger Thomas Leech. The frontage was designed by J. A. Gotch circa 1900. Along the right is the Northants Union Bank (now NatWest), built in 1901 and designed by Blackwell and Thompson. It was on the site previously occupied by Emerson's café and confectionery shop, demolished for road widening. (*Kettering Civic Society*)

Joseph Shaw, the coal merchant of Station Yard and Upper Field Street, rides his horse and cart along Newland Street in 1918. On the left he has just passed the premises of McClure and Co., the ladies and gents tailors. Ulster-born Mr McClure settled in Kettering in 1902 when the large block of buildings at the corner of Newland Street and Gold Street had been completed. His shop was double-fronted with a fitting room at the rear. On the right is the much-missed Mikado Café which later closed to make way for a travel bureau. (*Tony Smith*)

Behind these bollards at the Gold Street crossroads you can just see a helpful bobby directing traffic approaching from Montagu Street. This picture, probably taken in the 1920s, shows the street lamps erected on the island to illuminate the road sign. The police were no longer needed when traffic lights were introduced at this busy junction. (*Dick Fairey*)

Kettering was granted a weekly market in a charter by King Henry III on 17 March 1227. It came into the ownership of the Watson family of Rockingham Castle who, between 1646 and 1724, with the Montagu family, became joint Lords of the Manor. Market rights passed to Lord Sanders of Rockingham until 1881 when they were bought by the Local Board. (*Tony Smith*)

There used to be a line of houses at the front of the Market Place called Rotten Row, pulled down around 1785. The market, facing what was then called Turnpike Road, also had a cross plus stocks, a whipping post and pillory. The row of buildings pictured on Market Hill, which included the Albion Temperance Hotel at the bottom end, were demolished in the 1930s. (*Tony Smith*)

A photograph of Bakehouse Hill in the 1940s showing Theobald's, formerly J. Allen's bakehouse (built in 1865). Mr and Mrs Theobald took over the building in 1936, two years after opening their first shop and bakery in Hawthorn Road. The firm was famous for its cottage loaves and iced buns. In 1960 Mr Theobald retired and sold the business to Northampton bakers, Adams, which three years later amalgamated with United Bakeries. But the family name was retained, and during the 1960s Theobald's had four shops in Kettering, two in Wellingborough and one in Northampton – all served by the Kettering bakehouse, which moved round the corner to Lower Street when Bakehouse Hill was demolished in Phase One of the Gold Street redevelopment. Theobald's still have premises in Hawthorn Road. (*Tony Smith*)

A historic picture from August 1932 showing the former wooden blocked road being dug up on Bakehouse Hill and High Street, to be replaced with a Tarmac surface. The old blocks had deteriorated into a series of alarming pot-holes. Work was carried out during Kettering holiday week to cause as little disruption as possible, and crowds of shoppers gathered to watch the operation. This area is now part of the pedestrianised town centre. (*Robert Wharton*)

Broadway, pictured during the great blizzard of 1916 (see page 105). This impressive thoroughfare has housed many local luminaries, including Miss Edith Elworthy, daughter of brewer John Elworthy (1875), who married the Rev John Gray, curate of St Luke's in Alexandra Street (1909). Builder George Henson (1842-1907) lived at Sondes House on the corner of Headlands; Charles Speight began his photographic business here; shoemaker George Henry Jones was a resident at the turn of the century, and local historian and author Tony Ireson lived in Broadway as a child. Christine Stockburn generously presented Belle Vue, a beautiful house just off Broadway, to the town as the Stockburn Memorial Home in memory of her parents. For many years this property, at the end of Southlands, has been occupied by dentists. (*Kettering Civic Society*)

The Gaumont Pavilion in High Street shortly before it was closed for major redecorations, including the building of a small foyer, wide screen and remodelled frontage. Large crowds gathered for the official reopening on Friday 25 September 1953, by a certain starlet called Joan Collins, when the main feature was Genevieve, starring John Gregson and Dinah Sheridan. The 'Pav' was Kettering's first purpose-built cinema when it opened on Saturday 10 May 1913 on the site of John Newman's house. It seated 650 and the entrance had six marble steps illuminated by 48 electric lights. It was taken over in 1927 by the Gaumont-British Picture Corporation and two years later it was wired for sound, the first 'talkie' shown being The Perfect Alibi, starring Chester Morris. The cinema closed on Saturday 10 October 1959, and the last picture show was The Last Train from Gun Hill, with Kirk Douglas. The building was demolished in July 1960 to make way for the new store for Boots the Chemists. The Odeon in Gold Street (see front jacket) closed exactly a year after the Gaumont. (*Robert Wharton*)

A rare shot of Newland Street looking back towards the Gold Street crossroads circa 1931. The Gold Street and Montagu Street corners were built 1898-1900 by William Beesby and survive today. On the Montagu Street corner was Ernest Woodcock's store selling furnishing, upholstery, bedding, drapery and ladies' and children's wear. To its left was Henry Barlow's bakery and restaurant and opposite was the Northampton Rubber Company.
(*Robert Wharton*)

Newland Street was even more of a bottleneck in 1955 with two-way traffic including these wary cyclists. Woodcocks were still on the Montagu Street corner, and on the left were jeweller James Walker, the Co-op Permanent Building Society, and Lillian Worrall, a ladies' fashion shop run by two sisters and their brother. Next door you can just see H. Winstone's tobacco and newspaper shop.
(*Tony Smith*)

Roadworks are not just a modern phenomenon! This 1927 picture of Market Street shows the old Sun Hotel and former shops on the right, including A. A. Thornton, the well-known jewellers. Arthur Augustus Thornton (1879-1952) was born in Birmingham and came to Kettering in 1901 to work for watchmaker and jeweller Charles Usher in High Street. In 1909 he set up his own business in tiny premises towards the bottom of Market Street, then owned by Trustees of the old Grammar School. To its right was Hardy's, the saddlers, with Boots the Chemist on the corner (out of the picture). Mr Thornton's shop was so small he did repairs sitting in the window like the medieval craftsmen. He was a Liberal on the town council from 1913 to 1922, president of the Chamber of Trade and the Rotary Club in the 1930s, and later a county councillor. He was one of the first Aldermen in 1938, and in 1941 became Mayor and a JP. His son Pat and grandson Simon continued to develop and expand the family business, now based in the High Street next to the Royal Hotel. Sadly, Simon died on 13 January 1997 aged 61. (*Tony Smith*)

A church parade down Gold Street circa 1903 goes past shops (right) which included Charles George Symonds' jewellers, opened in 1897. Charles, who sold watches, clocks and optical instruments, spent three years on Kettering Council and was a director of Kettering Town Football Club. He spent many years as an optician at Kettering General Hospital and served the first ball at the opening of tennis courts off Headlands in July 1912! Born in Somerset, he spent 32 years in Kettering and died in 1928 aged 57. Gertrude Symonds took over the shop which remained a family business, and after 80 years in Gold Street the shop moved into the Newborough Centre in 1977. (*Robert Wharton*)

A view of High Street showing Bagley and Son, drapers, one of the most prominent traders in Kettering. Thomas Buckley Bagley was born in Newark in 1846 and died of a seizure in 1925. He learned his trade in the Nottingham area and opened his Kettering drapery in 1895. He was a Liberal, notable for his religious activities. He was a regular worshipper at the former Wesleyan Church in Silver Street and took an active role in services at the town's Men's Own Society. On the far right of the picture are the imposing Midland Bank chambers, built by the Leicestershire Banking Company in the early 1870s on a site previously occupied by ironmonger Thomas Leech. Its frontage was designed by J. A. Gotch circa 1900. (*Tony Smith*)

A section of Silver Street to the right of The Rising Sun circa 1920, including the butcher's shop run by Benjamin Mobbs, son of a Pytchley florist, and the Midland Railway parcels and enquiries office (later Chalkleys). The Liverpool Victoria Insurance Offices opened as the Liverpool Victoria Friendly Society in the 1880s. Alf Linnett was manager there for 31 years until he retired in 1928. In 1897 former schoolmistress Miss Clark of Weldon became the first lady collector. She toured villages in a pony and trap, always carrying a jack-knife and a loaded revolver for protection! Also pictured is The Grotto sweet shop, which later moved to Crispin Place (see page 130). (*Kettering Civic Society*)

The Liverpool Victoria Insurance Offices also feature (top right) in this 1931 view of Silver Street looking towards Newland Street. To the left of The Rising Sun is the Singer sewing machine shop, and the cycle store on the corner of Montagu Street belonged to Harry Taylor. About 100 bicycles were kept in the shop at prices ranging from 10 shillings (50p) to £8.10s. (£8.50), with more expensive models made to order. On the left is the Wesleyan Chapel (see page 37), which was pulled down for road widening two years after this photograph was taken. (*Robert Wharton*)

The Crown Inn, next to the Palace cinema, in Gold Street during the early 1930s. For three generations the pub sold Elworthy's beer, produced by the Crown Brewery behind in Tanners Lane. At one time the Elworthy family also owned the George Hotel and 15 country pubs. The company was bought in September 1931 by Marston, Thompson and Evershed of Burton-on-Trent, who used the brewery buildings as a depot but kept the Crown Inn open to sell its own ales. Both were to be demolished as part of the town centre redevelopment which also claimed the old Grammar School and Post Office buildings. (*Kettering Civic Society*)

## Wesleyan Chapel

Photographer Herbert Evans, who had a stationery shop on the Market Place, took this picture (below) of the imposing Wesleyan Chapel in Silver Street in 1928. The commanding building, erected in 1866 for £3,400, faced Dalkeith Place for almost 70 years and could seat 600 worshippers. The church (pictured left by Charles Speight), along with a row of shops and private houses behind it, was demolished by the urban council when the road was widened in 1933, and the Methodist Church in nearby School Lane was built as a replacement. The site of the Wesleyan Chapel is now occupied by a block of buildings which include Supervision and Ken Burton's sportswear shop.
(*Tony Smith and Robert Wharton*)

Victoria Terrace in Stamford Road, built in 1846 at the time of Queen Victoria's visit to Kettering. These houses, on the corner of Lawson Street (now the site of a disused petrol station), were typical of the mid-nineteenth century development in the town, lived in by workers of the rapidly expanding shoe trade. By 1860, limited areas near the town centre, such as School Lane and Hog Leys (now Horsemarket) had been developed, to be followed over the next decade by Headlands, Duke Street, Queen Street, Buccleuch Street and Mill Road. (*Kettering Civic Society*)

A 1907 Warren East picture of the Montagu Street cycle shop and works of William 'Peter' Hunt, Kettering's first motorist. Peter, a former foreman for Charles Wicksteed Engineers, was also one of the first to make and sell bicycles in the town. During 45 years of trading, he supplied thousands of machines, from old 'penny-farthings' and tricycles to motorcycles of the 1920s, and he even taught people how to ride them! He owned the first car in Kettering – an 1898 Benz Comfortable, a two-seater with a single cylinder engine and large solid rubber-tyred wheels. When it was seen in villages around Kettering, it caused great commotion and it was another 12 months before the next car appeared in town. Peter died on 11 March 1931, three years after retiring at the age of 72. His cycle depot is now occupied by White Gate florists and the Kettering Health Foods warehouse. Pictured here with an unusual shield-shaped radiator is an early Rover motor car. (*Robert Wharton*)

High Street in 1926 with Bakehouse Hill in the background. Here you can see the premises of Robert Bell, a Gotch and Saunders building erected in 1889. Bell, who died in 1935, came from Shropshire and opened his first hardware store in Market Harborough before succeeding the Noble family, ironmongers and bellhangers, in Kettering in 1910. He lived above the shop, which sold anything from guns to home-made paint, and was always on call for valued customers. Later, with John Billows as a partner, the business continued as an ironmongers until the shop was knocked down for the first phase of the central redevelopment which opened in 1969. (*Robert Wharton*)

The Gold Street crossroads in 1906, complete with a policeman controlling traffic. Dr John Allison's 'Argyll' motor car is parked in front of his Fuller House surgery. Dr Allison, whose previous premises were in Carrington Street, was an honorary surgeon at Kettering General Hospital, where he worked for no payment. He came to Kettering in 1889 when he was 26 and he was Medical Officer of Health to the urban council from 1906 to when he retired in 1930. Three years later, Fuller House was replaced by shops. (*Kettering Civic Society*)

Two refuse collectors load up their cart in Newland Street in the days before black bin-liners. The men, employed by Kettering Urban Council, needed to make many journeys to dispose of the rubbish left outside town centre shops. Today, in the age of the wheelie bin, this work is contracted out by the council. (*Kettering Civic Society*)

An old soldier, complete with a splendid bicycle, pauses to chat with a friend outside Vint's Electric Palace on the Market Place in 1911. In the background, outside the Geisha Dining and Tearooms, is an old-fashioned beat bobby. (*Kettering Civic Society*)

George Street pictured in the 1960s when there were petrol pumps outside Jewers' garage. In the early part of the century these premises were occupied by George Tunnicliffe and Company, decorators and plumbers. Mr Tunnicliffe was a well-known figure in the art world, and in 1921 was the sole member of Kettering Dryden Arts and Crafts Guild. The white building on the left belonged to fishmonger John Mobbs. The former president of the Northampton and District Fish Trade Association had worked in the shop since 1946 and took it over in 1968. Sadly he collapsed and died suddenly at his Barton Seagrave home in September 1986, only hours after taking early retirement and closing his shop for the last time (he was 63). The premises were converted to the Red Rose Indian Restaurant in the 1990s. Where the old petrol pumps stood is now a private yard next to the Cherry Tree, one of Kettering's oldest pubs dating back to 1629. (*Kettering Civic Society*)

A picture of children in Headlands just before World War I. This long, wide road, boasting large Victorian houses, was built during the 1860s and was formerly a private country lane. Draper Ernest Woodcock, last-factory boss Harry Mobbs, shoe tycoon William Timpson, and well-known builder, bellringer and clothing factory founder Frederic Wallis (1833-1886) of Wallis and Linnell, all lived here. William Timpson's home, Sunnylands, became St Peter's School in 1946 (see page 168) and Wallis's house, Lonsdale, together with Ferndale, have been old people's homes for many years. Christine Stockburn, youngest daughter of J. T. Stockburn (who ran the Mission House) lived in Headlands for 50 years. The playing fields at the far end were used for town sports before Bishop Stopford School was built in 1965 to replace the Parish Church School in Horsemarket (see page 65). (*Tony Smith*)

# 3. Buildings

Piccadilly Buildings in Sheep Street, designed by Charles Saunders of Gotch and Saunders, opened as a new shopping precinct in October 1926. The shops and offices, built to complement the library and art gallery opposite, consisted of five double-fronted and four single-fronted lock-up shops with offices and showrooms on the upper storey. New vaults at the corner replaced ones attached to the George Hotel. The first businesses were Messrs Swift and Presswell (dry cleaners), Marlow and Son (greengrocers), Henry Barlow and Son (bakers), Piccadilly Café, Laurence Photographers, M. E. Coles (ladies outfitters), Barnett and Soans (electrical engineers), Aston and Aston (women's clothiers) and the Northampton Town and County Benefit Building Society. Only M. E. Coles remains today. (*Robert Wharton*)

A closing down sale is advertised at Mill Direct Ltd on the corner of High Street and Meadow Road. The quarter-acre block of property fronting High Street was demolished in 1959 to make way for six shops in the town's largest commercial development since the war. The empty corner premises were torn down, along with a wine and spirit shop, ladies outfitters, The Farm Shop and an empty house in Meadow Road. The High Street was widened to bring the block in line with Freeman, Hardy & Willis. The new corner building became a Fine Fare supermarket during the 1960s and is now Peacocks clothing store (opposite McDonalds). (*Kettering Civic Society*)

Looking down Meadow Road in the late 1950s or early 1960s, before the road was widened. The large building on the left, of course, is the Granada cinema, formerly the Regal, opened by Earl Spencer on Boxing Day 1936, with 1,742 seats (1,200 in the stalls). Many stars came to the famous Regal Sunday Concerts, including Nat Gonella and Harry Farmer and his Hammond Organ. It became the Granada on 2 January 1948, and during the 1950s it hosted popular stage shows by Vera Lynn, Flanagan and Allen, Joe Loss, Geraldo, Jack Hylton and Henry Hall. In 1954 it was fitted with a wide screen and four-track stereo for CinemaScope, and 20 years later its last film was Zardos, starring Sean Connery and Charlotte Rampling. It is now the Gala Bingo Club owned by the Bass Leisure Group. (*Kettering Civic Society*)

Northall Street has seen major changes since the building of the town's inner ring road. The row of old houses in this 1958 picture no longer exists. The building with the tower was G. Stock and Son's leather factory (now Kettering Textiles Ltd). The premises on the right included the old Spring Gardens pub and Casburn's outdoor beerhouse. The building on the far left was the Victorian National School (also known as St Andrew's Church Institute), erected in 1859 on land donated by the Duke of Buccleuch. It was cleared for the new Tanners Lane service road in the mid-1970s. (*Kettering Civic Society*)

Old Tanners Lane was an amalgam of ancient houses, little cottages and commercial premises – some over 200 years old. It was a winding road linking Northall Street with Lower Street, passing the high wall fronting Beech House (see page 75). The old terraced houses pictured here in the 1950s were demolished, along with the Waggon and Horses pub at the top end and Jasmine House, once the home of Thomas Henry Gotch, at the bottom corner. The wider, realigned Tanners Lane, opened to traffic in February 1975, is now a one-way access road to the Newlands' multi-storey car park. Historic Beech Cottage was saved, but lost its front garden to the new road (see page 74). (*Kettering Civic Society*)

The former Stamford Road Schools in Montagu Street in 1908. The mixed and infants schools, catering for 660 and 416 pupils respectively, were designed by John Alfred Gotch and built by Alfred Barlow. The Right Hon. A.H. Acland performed the opening ceremony in December 1892. By the 1930s, council schools had been reorganised and Stamford Road Senior became boys only. (*Tony Smith*)

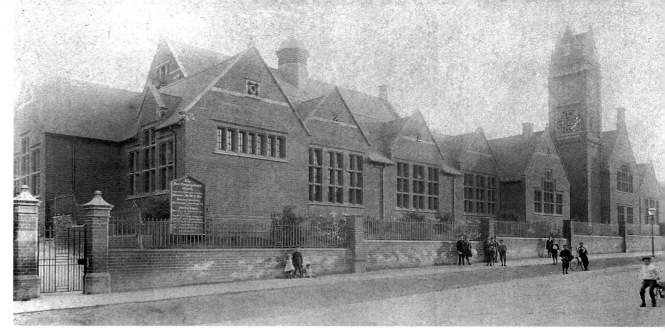

The headmaster's office was at the top of the tower on the left. The school magazine was also called *The Tower*, and a drawing of it decorated the cover. A £75,000 extension was opened in 1964 when it was known as Kettering Secondary School for Boys. In 1975 it catered for first and second-year pupils of Kettering Boys School, which closed in 1981. It is now the William Knibb Centre, providing offices for the youth and education services. (*Robert Wharton*)

A rare picture of Montagu Street taken in 1908. On the far left is Alf Tutty's agricultural ironmongers, which stood next to Robinson's garage. Tutty's, previously in High Street, became Tutty and Payne in the 1930s. The large stone building was the farmhouse of William Hircock, who died in 1909 at the age of 94. This was later the site of the KICS Lutona shop. The cart on the right is outside the site where the Central Hall was built. Out of the picture to the right would have been the Conservative Club, which opened on 17 December 1888. (*Dick Fairey*)

## Althorp's 'chippie'

This empty ramshackle old house in the middle of Market Street is pictured in January 1923. It was last a fish and chip shop run by fishmonger Henry Thomas Althorp, and before him, popular butcher George Gray. The building, just above the Golden Lion pub (see page 132), was demolished in 1925 for road widening and to make way for the entrance to the new fire station. (*Kettering Civic Society*)

The Town Hall and Corn Exchange (right) on the Market Place in 1903. The brick building with stone facings was erected in 1853 from designs by Northampton architect Francis Edmund Law (who also designed the old Grammar School in Gold Street) for £2,950. It had a large market room and an upper chamber for council meetings, and in the evenings it was used for concerts, lectures, exhibitions, balls, shows and private functions. It became an electric theatre seating 600 people in 1909 when London-based Leo Vint acquired the building as part of his chain of early picture palaces (see page 106). For many years it was the largest hall in town, hosting political and other public meetings – and, for a time, the top floor was Kettering's library. The urban council bought it in 1926 to use as a covered market. (*Tony Smith*)

The Royal Hotel, circa 1914. Formerly the White Hart, its name was changed by landlord Henry Draper after a 'comfort stop' there by Queen Victoria and Prince Albert in 1844. They stayed just 15 minutes before continuing by coach to Burghley House, Stamford. Four triumphal arches were erected in Kettering in their honour, and 1,100 Sunday School children were among those who lined the streets to welcome them. Nine years earlier Charles Dickens stayed at the hotel, which was rebuilt in 1878 and was once owned by the Duke of Buccleuch. (*Robert Wharton*)

## Kettering Parish Church

Kettering's Parish Church of SS Peter and Paul, built of Barnack stone, is the oldest building in town and one of the most impressive in the county. Its 178-ft spire has been a landmark for miles down the centuries. The much-restored chancel dates from around 1300, the rest being built between 1450 and 1500. The tower had 10 bells, three of them cast by Thomas Eayre, who had a bell foundry in the town during the mid-eighteenth century. On the south chapel wall is a small brass of Edmund Sawyer, builder of the almshouses opposite the Manor House gardens, who died in 1630. The stained glass west window is a memorial to Canon Henry Lindsay (see next page) and there is a bronze tablet on the west wall of the south aisle in memory of the nineteenth century artist John Trivett Nettleship. (*Tony Smith*)

An early photograph of St Mary's Church in Fuller Street, consecrated on 2 February 1895 by the Bishop of Peterborough, the Rt Rev. Mandell Creighton. Previously worshippers had used the 'Tin Church', an iron building erected on the site and last used by a chapel in Filbeach, London. The new building was designed by J. A. Gotch and built by Henshaws of Wellingborough. The foundation stone was laid on 10 June 1893 by Miss Katherine Lindsay, daughter of the late Canon Henry Lindsay, former rector of Kettering (1863-92). The church was deliberately set in the heart of a thickly populated area to take 'spiritual care' to the working classes and the poor. It boasted a medieval font which came from Sibbertoft Church, where Canon Lindsay once served. A 75th anniversary service in 1970 was conducted by the Rt Rev. Cyril Eastaugh, Bishop of Peterborough. (*Dick Fairey*)

A crowd of disbelieving townsfolk gathered in Gold Street on the morning of Sunday, 29 November 1964, as workers reduced the old Grammar School to rubble. This fine Victorian Gothic stone building, complete with headmaster's house, was used as a school until 1913 when its 50 pupils moved to larger premises in Bowling Green Road (see next page). It then became the house and surgery of Dr Daniel Drake-Lee until the early 1930s, when the doctor built a new surgery in Lower Street next to the Post Office and went to live in what is now Satra House in Rockingham Road. For its final 20 years the old school was the Council Surveyor's Department, before being replaced by a characterless row of shops. This picture was taken in the 1920s. The datestone on the top left tower is in the Manor House Museum. (*Tony Smith*)

This neo-Georgian building in Bowling Green Road (now the council offices) cost £13,375 and was designed by Gotch and Saunders. It was shared by Kettering Grammar School and the High School in 1913. Lessons were staggered to keep the boys and girls apart, and they even had separate playgrounds! (*Tony Smith*)

A close-up of the frontage to the old schools. Kettering Grammar School moved to a new building in Windmill Avenue in 1963. It became Kettering Boys School after comprehensive reorganisation in 1975 but was forced to close in 1994 because of falling rolls. The High School moved to Lewis Road, became Southfield School for Girls and is now self-funded. (*Robert Wharton*)

Kettering General Hospital, pictured shortly after the turn of the century, celebrates its centenary in 1997. The building in Rothwell Road, erected in 1896/97 and enlarged in 1902/03 from designs by Gotch and Saunders, cost about £18,000 in total and was officially opened on 30 October 1897 by Lord Althorp. It was built on five acres of ground donated by the Duke of Buccleuch, and initially had three wards providing 23 beds. It also had a single operating theatre, offices and domestic departments. The running costs were paid mostly by voluntary subscription, and of its income of £1,534 in 1898/99, £700 came from collections in workshops and factories. It was run by a board of governors, with John Turner Stockburn as president. (*Kettering Civic Society*)

The women's ward at Kettering General Hospital in 1907. Visits to patients were allowed only on Fridays from 2pm to 3.30pm and Sundays from 2pm to 3pm, with patients permitted to have only four visitors on one day. In the hospital's first year there were 179 admissions – 55 women, 75 men and 49 children – and their average stay was around 32 days. (*Tony Smith*)

The hospital's resources were stretched during World War I when the Government provided extra funds for the treatment of wounded soldiers. Tented wards with 60 extra beds were erected in the gardens to cope with the increase in patient numbers, and by the end of the war almost a thousand men had been treated. This picture is dated around 1905. (*Tony Smith*)

*Kettering and District General Hospital.*

## Dryland Memorial

The Dryland Memorial outside the public library in Sheep Street was erected in 1907. Designed by John Alfred Gotch, it was a tribute to Dr John Winter Dryland, who came to Kettering from Newbury in 1857 and became Medical Officer for the Board of Guardians and adviser for the workhouse. He was active in promoting the Isolation Hospital (later Rockingham Road Hospital) and Kettering General Hospital, both built in 1897. The memorial was a drinking fountain with two horse troughs and a lower trough for dogs. With the demise of horse transport, the troughs were removed in 1947, but after a campaign by Kettering Civic Society new £4,000 troughs were unveiled in March 1995 by the doctor's great granddaughter, Professor Katherine Dryland, who flew from the USA to perform the ceremony. (*Tony Smith*)

Kettering Public Library was opened on 7 May 1904. It cost over £8,000 to build and was designed by John Alfred Gotch from no less than 79 designs submitted to him. Eleven firms tendered for the work, four in Kettering, four in Leicester, two in Wellingborough and one in Rothwell. The contract was won by the Kettering Co-operative Builders, who used rich sandstone bricks with Ketton stone windows and a roof of Collyweston slates. It included a vestibule with mosaic flooring, lending library and reference library. The reading room sat 100 people, 56 at tables and 44 at nine newspaper stands. The library had a stock of 6,358 books, but the new shelves could accommodate 30,000. A new duplicate ticket was introduced to enable readers to borrow two books at a time. (*Tony Smith*)

Dalkeith Press, in Dalkeith Place, was a well-known printing works, founded in 1925 by the late Mr H. E. Cox. When taken over by millionaire John Nash in June 1972 it employed just 23 people. In 1955 two shops over 100 years old were demolished for an extension to the works. They belonged to cobbler Bert Cox, who moved to Eskdaill Street, and butcher Hubert Salter, who retired because of ill health. The chimney being repaired in the picture belonged to the Kettering Dairy, established in 1901, which processed milk delivered daily by local village farmers. The premises (seen top right on page 103) included a shop which sold milk and milk products, such as sour milk cheeses and pasteurised cream. The building – now gone – stood on the site occupied by the Tunks and Tisdall dairy, set up in 1777. (*Kettering Civic Society*)

The first council houses on the Stamford Road estate were built in 1921. Pictured here is the first tenant, James Hough, a 29-year-old engineer with Messrs Childs and Wright in Havelock Street. The three-bedroomed house had a living room containing a cooking range, and there was a good scullery where the copper was heated by gas. Some 171 houses were built and 139 added later, but streets were still to be named when this picture was taken. The lorry belonged to Walter Keach, who ran a coal merchants in Crown Street. (*Kettering Civic Society*)

The George Hotel in Sheep Street in 1915, with a wall placard (far left) announcing the loss of the great Cunard passenger liner, the Lusitania. A total of 1,201 men, women and children died when the ship was sunk off the Old Head of Kinsale after being twice torpedoed by the German submarine U-20. The coroner hit out at this 'wilful and wholesale murder' by the Kaiser, whose men had contravened international agreements. Many US citizens were on board and the disaster was among many factors which brought America into the war. (*Dick Fairey*)

Horsemarket in the early 1920s before the premises of leather firm G. H. Frecknall and Co. (in distance) were demolished for road widening. On the right is the former Boys' National School, opened in February 1873 on a site donated by the Duke of Buccleuch. It began with 200 boys and three staff, kept going by voluntary contributions and an initial fee of a penny a week per pupil. After 50 years it became the Parish Church School, a mixed secondary modern. By the late 1950s it was considered overcrowded, outdated and badly sited for its 270 pupils. It was replaced by Bishop Stopford School in Headlands in 1965. The derelict building was demolished in September 1970 and is now a taxi rank and gardens. The Woolpack Inn in the centre of the picture is now a theme pub called Henry's. (*Kettering Civic Society*)

## The Old White Horse

The Old White Horse in High Street, pictured just before
it was demolished in 1905. It was rebuilt at a site to the
right, on the corner of Huxloe Place, and was very popular
with *Evening Telegraph* journalists, whose offices were
behind. The hotel closed on 24 November 1959, and the
last landlord was Ron Thornton. The building, with its
impressive spire, was taken over by Montagu Burton, the
men's tailors, and when it opened as a shop on
23 February 1962, free suits were given away to the first
six old-age pensioners. (*Dick Fairey*)

The New White Horse Inn in High Street was a popular pub and one of the oldest in town. The last pint was pulled on Tuesday 28 May 1957 when 60 regulars said goodbye to landlord Bill Collier and his wife. Other taverns which have vanished over the last century or so include The Three Crowns, Montagu Street, The Waggon and Horses, Tanners Lane, The Boot and Crown, Bakehouse Hill, The Royal Oak, Meeting Lane (later rebuilt as The Crispin), The Half Moon, Market Street (next to the old Sun Inn), The Duke's Arms, Market Street, The Duke of Wellington, Horsemarket, The Cross Keys Inn, Lower Street (later The King's Arms), The Nag's Head, West Street (later Dixons shoe shop), The Red Lion and Fleur de Lys, Newland Street, The Vine and Hare and Hounds, Rockingham Road (now Sainsbury's superstore), and The Old White Horse, High Street (now Burton's menswear store). The New White Horse used to be known as The Lord Nelson. On the right is the Electric Pavilion, later the Gaumont cinema. (*Dick Fairey*)

## Victoria Picture Palace

A fine view of the Victoria Picture Palace in Gold Street during the 1920s. This Gotch and Saunders building opened as the Victoria Hall on 17 December 1888, when Kettering Choral Society (still going!) performed Handel's *Messiah*. The emporium could accommodate 1,000 people, and seating could be removed for dinners, dances and bazaars. Theatrical shows were booked by music shop owner Alf Bailey, whose own string band played from the pit. It reopened as a cinema on Monday 23 August 1920 after renovations paid for by a syndicate of local businessmen. The balcony had a sloping floor and it boasted tip-up seats in crocodile leather. The upper floor was converted to the Victoria Tea Rooms in December that year. It became the super new Odeon on Saturday 19 September 1936, part of a chain owned by Oscar Deutsch, and the first film was *Strike Me Rich* with Eddie Cantor. It closed down in 1960, and for a year became a bingo hall, but was demolished in 1974 to make way for the Newborough Centre. (*Kettering Civic Society*)

The demolition of the old police station in London Road at the end of the 1960s. This impressive building was erected in 1851, enlarged in 1894, and again in August 1909 when county council chairman Colonel S. G. Stopford-Sackville officially opened the new court, used for the first time as petty sessions. On 14 September 1971, Home Secretary Reginald Maudling opened the new £196,000 station, courthouse and probation office complex, built a little further left of the original site. (*Tony Smith*)

## The USF Club

This Victorian building in Meeting Lane used to be the old Griffin public house until it closed shortly after World War I. It remained empty until 1921, when it was bought by the United Services Fund and turned into an ex-servicemen's club, which survives today. After the war the USF had received £1,287 from a share of army canteen profits – five bob (25p) for each of the 5,000 Kettering men who served. With this money it bought Beech House (see page 75), but soon sold it when it could not afford the conversion costs. In this picture, taken from the Toller Church Sunday School rooms, a bicycle is leaning on a bricked-up corner, which later became the club's main entrance. Above this door you can still see the name 'Griffin' engraved in stone. It was built on the site of the former Royal Oak pub, destroyed by fire one Sunday night in September 1889. In June 1992 another fire badly damaged the first floor of the USF Club, but fortunately the 40 customers within fled to safety. (*Dick Fairey*)

Anyone for tennis? You may know Westfield as Kettering's former museum at the bottom of West Street, but this double-bayed Victorian house, with fine gardens, was once the private home of solicitor Mr A. C. D. Holmes of Lamb and Holmes (who still have an office in West Street). It was opened as a museum by the Duke of Buccleuch on 15 June 1961 and had four display rooms for Saxon remains, natural history, a butterfly and moth collection, and boots and shoes loaned by Mr J. Thornton of Northampton Technical College. Prized exhibits included samples of the last 'pigs' made by Kettering Iron and Coal Company and the old Geddington fire engine. Former borough librarian John Burden was the curator, with Mr F. V. Lyle as his assistant. It closed in October 1986, to be replaced three years later by the Manor House Museum in Sheep Street. Westfield House remained empty until February 1996 when work began to convert it into flats for the elderly. The house had the dubious distinction of being the first private home in Kettering to have a flush toilet installed! (*Dick Fairey*)

Speight's corner at the junction of Bowling Green Road and London Road in 1912. Charles Speight, who came from Rugby, was the town's best-known commercial photographer. His studio, erected in 1886, was a Gotch building known to some as Gotch's folly. Built in stone with big display windows, its most striking feature was the baroque balcony on the first floor corner, which survives today. Hundreds of children had their portrait photos taken by Speight or his daughter Helen, and newlyweds would visit his studio after the ceremony. Many of Speight's photographs were used on picture postcards. The building is now occupied by a dress agency. (*John Darker*)

Workers leave the former Freeman, Hardy & Willis factory in Mill Road in 1957. The Victorian building was first owned by the Kettering Boot and Shoe Manufacturing Company in 1871. It began as a modest factory in Albert Street, but was later enlarged to have frontages in Thorngate Street and Mill Road. By World War I it was taken over by the Leicester-based Freeman, Hardy & Willis, which sold its shoes in its chain of 500 shops. Weekly production reached a peak of 14,000 pairs of men's and boy's shoes, with more than 400 workers in the 1940s and 50s. The factory closed in September 1959, was later used by Anglian Lamps, and was demolished in March 1996 to make way for a 55-bed care home for the elderly. (*Tony Smith*)

Historic Beech Cottage in Tanners Lane, before the bulldozers robbed Tony Ireson of his lovely garden in the town centre revamp of 1975. The picturesque building, with its stone walls and carved gargoyles, was originally part of Beech House Farm, dating from around 1700. In 1929 it was modernised by the Elworthy family as a home for the manager of their nearby brewery. Tony and his wife Rene moved in during 1947, and the *Evening Telegraph* journalist was proud of his garden retreat with its flowers, vegetables, fruit trees, greenhouse and old well. In 1975 Tony won the battle with the council to save his quaint home, but lost his garden to a new service road, and his cottage now faces the Newlands' multi-storey car park. The full story is told in his book *Old Kettering and its Defenders*. (*Tony Ireson*)

Beech House in old Tanners Lane was a dominant feature for over 250 years. Dating from Queen Anne, the oldest part was built in 1704. It was home to the Wright family for four generations and had connections with the Stockburn, Wallis and Butlin families. The Elworthys, who ran the Crown Brewery facing it, also lived there. In the 1950s it was turned into nine flats by Charles Eayrs, brother-in-law of Tony Ireson of nearby Beech Cottage. The house was sold to Kettering Council in 1971 and was demolished in 1975 to make way for the Newborough Centre, despite a public inquiry and a campaign to save the listed building launched by Kettering Civic Society. (*Kettering Civic Society*)

A chapter in Kettering's history came to an end when the old baths closed on 18 December 1983. The town first had an outdoor pool in the early 1800s, financed by local shoe makers. It was taken over by the urban council in 1901 and was divided in two to create an outdoor and indoor pool, which opened on 26 March 1915. Between the wars the baths were used for political meetings, dances and even boxing matches. In 1968 a life-saving club was set up by resident instructress Miss Mary Bonham, who taught thousands of Kettering youngsters how to swim. In the mid-1970s plans were drawn up to build a new, modern pool off Deeble Road as part of a proposed leisure complex on the Ise Lodge estate, but the scheme was ditched because of spending cuts. A new £770,000 pool eventually opened on the London Road car park on 10 January 1984, complete with a sauna and solarium. The old baths (in Bath Lane) were demolished in November 1985, their 110 ft chimney being the last to go.

(*Tony Smith*)

# 4. Transport

A Leyland 36 hp double-decker bus stops outside the former Rockingham Road School in Dryden Street to pick up passengers in the 1920s. The vehicle was one of 37 buses acquired by United Counties after taking over the Wellingborough Motor Omnibus Company in September 1921. In the distance is the distinctive frontage of the old Wesleyan Church (erected in 1893) on the corner of Rockingham Road and Regent Street (now the Salvation Army Citadel). For any bus buffs out there, this particular vehicle was in service from March 1921 to June 1929. It had a livery of ultramarine blue with white windows, and its chassis number was 10707. Honest. (*Kettering Civic Society*)

A Leyland RAF single-decker bus fills up with petrol from the Pratts pump at the old United Counties bus garage in Havelock Street in 1923. The vehicle travelled the No. 6 route which ran daily from Kettering to Northampton, making stops at Broughton, the Red House and Moulton. It was withdrawn from service in December 1927, its body going to the Leicester Co-operative Society and the chassis to J. C. Huxley of Whitchurch. The former garage was built in the grounds of Rockingham House at a cost of £3,100 by Smith, Edmunds and Company of Havelock Street. The garage could house only 10 vehicles, but was used for 13 years before being replaced by the depot in Northampton Road. (*Kettering Civic Society*)

Now, here's a photograph for all motoring enthusiasts – an early Model T Ford converted for use as a delivery lorry. It is parked in a jitty opposite the Liverpool Victoria Insurance Offices in Silver Street (see page 34) circa 1910. The vehicle belonged to fruiterer and greengrocer Alfred William Johnson, formerly of Market Place and Montagu Street. (*Kettering Civic Society*)

The humble horse and cart was the main mode of transport for deliveries to and from local factories early this century. These are outside the Albert Street premises of the old 'Kettering Boot Company' (full name Kettering Boot and Shoe Manufacturing Company). It was founded in 1871 by Henry Standley, who died in 1911 (see page 73). (*Robert Wharton*)

Lorry drivers of R. Bagshaw and Co. with their vehicles after the firm went over to haulage. From their garage in Tanners Lane, Bagshaws were among the first to run charabancs and buses in the 1920s and 30s. The firm was founded by former fish and poultry merchant Richard Bagshaw, whose sons were Percy and Bert. As a young man, Bert sold wet fish from a barrow he pushed through Kettering. (*Tony Smith*)

Bagshaws charabancs were popular for day outings to the seaside or the country. Here they are setting out from the workhouse in London Road (now St Mary's Hospital) on 8 June 1920. They drove to Oundle via Weldon and Benefield, returning by a different route through Thrapston and Cranford. There were two trips using three charas, one at 1pm and the other at 5pm. It was the first outing of its kind from the Kettering Poor Law Institute (its full title), and for many inmates it was their first-ever ride in a petrol-driven vehicle. (*Kettering Civic Society*)

Kettering's first fatal road crash happened in 1907. The saloon car was owned by Viscount Downe of Dingley Hall, near Market Harborough, and was on its way to London driven by chauffeur Frederick Frost, with his wife and baby daughter Delia as passengers. The car left the road in darkness at the notorious junction of Pytchley Road and Wellingborough Road, killing Delia. Kettering's first serious crash was in May 1901 when Harry Brampton's motor tricycle smashed into a tree near the village of Weekley. (*Kettering Civic Society*)

This Buick was taking a Kettering party to greyhound racing at Northampton on Saturday 18 August 1928 when it was in collision with a Humber at the Overstone-Moulton crossroads.. Its driver, Mr J. Harris, was unhurt, but passengers George Roberts and Mr G. W. Althorpe were taken to Northampton Hospital, and the Humber driver, Sywell farmer Harold Brown, was thrown through the windscreen. Mr Roberts, of Pollard Street in Kettering, had six stitches in a head wound, but Mr Althorpe, of Wellington Street, had a displaced knee and was able to go on to the dog racing! Both vehicles were write-offs. In the picture the man without a hat is Mr C. F. Goddard of Kettering, and the man in the trilby is garage proprietor Thomas Wallis of London Road. (*Dick Fairey*)

Two short-bodied Leyland Lion buses are seen parked outside the Library and Art Gallery in Sheep Street in the late 1920s. The first 18 of these famous single-deckers were delivered to United Counties in 1927, bringing the company's fleet to 97 buses. The Leyland Lions were one of the earliest vehicles purpose-built for passengers rather than for freight. At the time they were considered very advanced, and they gave reliable public service for over a quarter of a century. But some people still depended on the horse and cart, seen here outside the George Hotel at the top of Northampton Road.  (*Kettering Civic Society*)

Local farmers pictured with the Raunds bus at the old Cattle Market (now London Road car park) in 1922. In the distance are the Congregational Chapel, built in 1893, and the Corn Market Hall, erected by the council in 1913 for £1,300. The Cattle Market moved from Market Place to London Road in 1880 and remained there until 1965 when it was replaced by a modern market in Northfield Avenue. This closed – after more than a century of operation – in March 1992. (*Kettering Civic Society*)

Yes, it's those Bagshaw charabancs again, returning the ladies and gentlemen to the workhouse after their afternoon excursion (see page 81). About 140 inmates enjoyed the trip, along with many staff and numerous visitors, including Board of Guardians members Miss Wilmot, Mr H. Loasby and Mr F. W. Roughton. Passengers had doors on each side, got in and out with the help of a footboard and handrail and, if it rained, there was even a hood at the back which could be pulled over. The following week Bagshaws took 53 local blind people on their annual picnic by the river at Bedford. They left at noon and arrived at 2.30pm but took four hours to come back, arriving in Kettering at 11pm after a stop in Rushden.

(*Kettering Civic Society*)

Kettering's first motor bus appeared in 1898 and was owned by Jack Lee, a former engineer at Charles Wicksteed and Co. of Digby Street. The service ran from the Royal Hotel to Rothwell and Desborough carrying up to 14 passengers. As you can see from the photograph, the bus offered scant protection against the weather for the driver. Sadly, the service made little money and ceased about 1903. It wasn't until 10 years later that the area's first bus company, Wellingborough Motor Omnibus Company (later United Counties), was formed. (*Kettering Civic Society*)

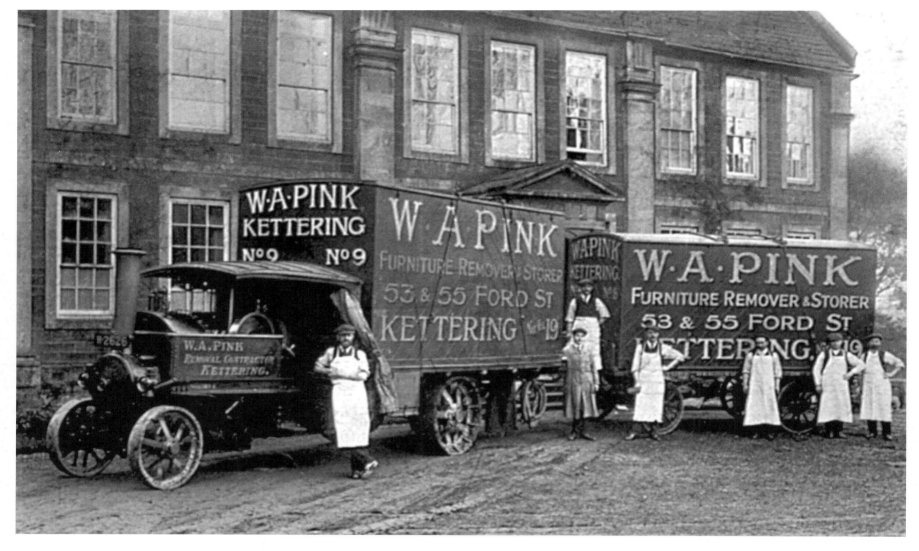

A Foden steam lorry belonging to furniture removers W. A. Pink pictured outside Orlingbury Hall shortly after it was purchased in 1910. Yorkshire-born Mr Pink originally set up as a coal merchant with a donkey and cart trading from premises in Montagu Street in 1885. He began Kettering's first removal business in Ford Street three years later, and his first vans were horse-drawn. In 1944 he took on John Jones from Darlington, and even after Mr Pink died in 1953, aged 90, the firm still traded as Pink and Jones. It was taken over by Bartley Industries in 1973, and in April 1996 was bought by Harrison and Rowley of Bedford. It is now based in Telford Way and is known as Britannia Pink and Jones. The old steam lorry in the picture worked for 22 years until it was scrapped! (*Tony Smith*)

# 5. Events

Children on the Co-op float pictured after the Kettering Hospital Parade of 1908. Competitors assembled at the Manor House Field, and those in the horse parade at the Cattle Market in London Road, before marching through the town to the Church Institute ground in Garfield Street, where judging took place. There were prizes for the best decorated cycle, best floral display, and best fancy 'get-up', with or without cycles. A full programme of sports events was held, including half-mile relay races, a cycle obstacle race and tug-of-war. In the evening there was a male adult school choir contest, won by Kettering Friends' Adult School. (*Kettering Civic Society*)

It was one of the most memorable days in Kettering's history when Col. William Frederick Cody – alias 'Buffalo Bill' – rode into town. On 19 September 1903 his spectacular Wild West Roadshow was performed in Bayes Field, off Rothwell Road – where the Do-It-All store and the *Evening Telegraph* now stand. Four special trains brought 800 genuine cowboys and Indians and an incredible 500 horses to the seven-acre site. The vast arena had covered seating for 14,000 people and hundreds of spectators from nearby villages arrived by carriers' carts, bicycles, traps and wagonettes. Two special electric lamps (an early form of floodlighting) were used for the evening performance. The colourful show featured re-creations of well-known Wild West incidents, such as a stagecoach hold-up, cowboys' round-up, an attack on a train, and Indian war dances. There were also equestrian feats, a warlike pageant and military exercises by veteran cavalrymen. The cost of entrance ranged from a shilling (5p) to stand, to 7s. 6d. (37p) for a box seat.

Charles Wicksteed and his daughter Hilda had a tremendous reception from 2,600 youngsters as they roamed his newly-opened park during Children's Day on 9 September 1921. The tea party was a treat for the children of Kettering club members, who donated the clocktower on the canteen in Wicksteed Park. There were two main processions to Dalkeith Place, from where they marched in one body, four abreast, to the park, carrying their cups and saucers. There they were handed bags of bread and butter and cake. The children all shouted 'Hurrah' when Mr Wicksteed appeared. About 400 adults, including local bands, ambulance and general workers, had their own tea. Entertainment included puppets, a conjuror, Punch and Judy Show and Pierrots, and children were charged a penny for a boat ride on the lake. (*Kettering Civic Society*)

The Kettering Hospital Carnival parade makes its way along a wet Montagu Street on 12 June 1926. It is led by the striking mounted figure of 'John Bull', alias Trevor Spencer, dressed in a splendid old English costume, complete with frills and a Union Jack waistcoat. Following him is 'Ye Olde Stagecoach and Four' from the Peacock Hotel in Northampton. Torrential rain threatened to ruin the fête at Wicksteed Park that afternoon. An official announced at 6pm that the fête would make a loss of £50, but the sun broke through soon after and, by 8pm, another 1,500 people had each paid their threepence admission. Only two events were abandoned – a gymnastics display and a performance by pupils of Miss Betty Brooks' dance school. (*Dick Fairey*)

## Kettering Feast

The Peacock scenic ride at Kettering Feast in June 1923. Since the fourth century, the week-long fair has been staged in the town from the first Sunday after St Peter's Day. For most of the last century the leaseholder on Northampton Road has been the firm of Charles and John Thurston, the most famous of fairground families dating from the 1840s. Charles introduced the first moving pictures to Kettering people with his 1901 bioscope show. When he died in 1928, his son John Henry Thurston took over. He was born at Kettering Feast and attended every year until his death on 25 April 1972, aged 76. Pictured here with his grandson John in 1960, he introduced the custom of giving children free admission to the rides on one day of the week. (*Tony Smith*)

A procession from the Corn Market Hall to the Parish Church on Wednesday 18 May 1927 as part of the week-long Kettering Anglo-Catholic Congress in preparation for a national congress in London. Daily meetings were held at the hall addressed by well-known personalities in the movement and Benedictine preachers. A special High Mass was held in the church for the banner-bearing choirs and servers of St Michael's, St Luke's and St Mary's churches. Following those in the picture were local ministers in gold vestments, the Revs. C. B. Lucas (celebrant), F. I. Ware (deacon) and P. R. Greville (sub-deacon), and the Rt Rev. Bishop O'Rorke, wearing a gold cape and jewelled mitre. After the mass, visiting priests had lunch at the George Hotel. The procession is pictured here by the Cattle Market in London Road which then possessed two ornate entrances. (*Dick Fairey*)

General Booth, veteran head of the Salvation Army, visited the Mission House in Lower Street on Thursday 18 July 1907. After stops at Rushden, Higham Ferrers and Wellingborough in the morning, he addressed a civic reception at the Victoria Hall, Kettering, where there was a brass band to welcome him. He was entertained at the Mission House by draper Mr John Turner Stockburn, J.P. (on steps).
(*Kettering Civic Society*)

As the General left for Peterborough at 6pm, he stood waving in his car as crowds cheered him along the High Street to Bowling Green Road and London Road. During a previous visit in 1898, he spoke in the old Mission Hall (later the Co-op Hall). His third and final visit to Kettering was in September 1911 at the age of 83.
(*Tony Smith*)

The county forgot its war worries when King George VI and Queen Elizabeth visited Kettering, Corby, Wellingborough and Northampton on 4 March 1943. The royal couple spent 50 minutes at the Kaycee clothing factory in Dryden Street where they chatted with some of the 900 employees. Here they are both greeted by factory manager Harold Taylor, with the Mayor, Alderman J. P. Dainty, on the left and town clerk John Chaston (centre). (*Robert Wharton*)

Nurses from Kettering General Hospital, in their red cloaks, form a guard of honour as the King and Mr Taylor cross the road from the gents' factory to the ladies' factory. Thousands of people, including more than 1,200 schoolchildren, waved flags, cheered and sang 'There'll always be an England' as the King and Queen left the factory. Because of wartime restrictions, the local press referred to Kaycee as a 'Midlands factory'.
Two hundred workers lost their jobs when the 80-year-old factory closed in 1975.
(*Robert Wharton*)

Kettering's public library was presented to the town by the well-known benefactor Andrew Carnegie, who broke tradition by officially opening the building in Sheep Street himself on Saturday 7 May 1904. The town's first library and newsroom had been opened by the then council chairman J. T. Stockburn on 2 March 1896 at the old Corn Exchange on Market Place. When it was transferred to Silver Street in October 1901 it contained 1,660 books. However, demand was such that the urban council chairman Alfred Webb and accountant Andrew Roscoe approached Mr Carnegie on the town's behalf. After opening the library Mr Carnegie attended the official 'switch on' of the new electricity power station and refuse destructor in Rockingham Road, which provided light for 30 arc lamps in the town's streets. (*Kettering Civic Society*)

This archway at the entrance to Headlands celebrated the coronation of King George V in 1911. The letters G.R. were illuminated by electric lamps. The council gave awards for the best decorated street, house and shop in each of the town's five wards. A large canopy was erected on Market Hill festooned with flags and streamers, and a Gothic arch stood at the London Road end of Broadway with a portrait of the King. (*Kettering Civic Society*)

Hundreds of Kettering schoolchildren assembled in the Manor House field at 11am to take part in the coronation pageant and procession through the town. In the afternoon they enjoyed a tea party in Headlands and Broadway. The day had begun at 6 am with an hour-long peal of bells at the Parish Church, but heavy rain in the evening meant an early stop to various sports events. (*Winnie Bailey*)

Silver Street, Kettering. Coronation. 1911.

There was a double arch at the top of Gold Street and single ones in Montagu Street, Silver Street and Newland Street. The Gas Company lit up those in Gold Street and Montagu Street. Shops and houses were also decorated, along with the library and the George Hotel. In Newland Street there were special window displays at Woodcocks, Barlow and Son, Phillips and the Co-op store. All the arches in principal streets were erected by Mr G. Tunnicliffe. The urban council provided a 40 ft flagpole near the library. A total of £603 was raised by voluntary subscription to help pay for the festivities. (*Kettering Civic Society*)

A popular fundraising event during the 1920s was Hospital Week, when a series of activities, including an annual fête and carnival, were organised to bring in extra revenue for Kettering General Hospital. The men with the brushes, pictured outside Brakes in Gold Street, are collecting the proceeds from the 'mile of pennies' placed by shoppers along a freshly-painted white line on the pavement. The line would go right round the town centre. (*Tony Smith*)

'Miles of pennies'

Two more 'miles of pennies', one (right) on the Market Place and the other with two policemen looking on (above), presumably to make sure none of the coins goes missing mysteriously! The idea – often described as the thin bronze line – was also borrowed for other events in the town to raise money for Armistice Day or for the war effort. (above *Kettering Civic Society* and right *Dick Fairey*)

A troop of boy scouts prepare for inspection after a Sunday parade during the 1920s. This picture was taken from the upper floor of the Cross Keys Restaurant, erected in 1880 and named after the manorial sign of the Abbot of Peterborough and his successors, part holders of the Manor of Kettering. It was the HQ of the Free Gardeners, the Manchester Oddfellows and other societies, and a recognised venue for parties, dances and other functions. The restaurant, run by Dick Tarry since 1903, could seat 180, split into first and second class dining rooms and ladies' dining rooms, and boasted a billiard room and ballroom with a spring floor. When Mr Tarry retired in April 1932 it was sold for £2,950 to Ernest Wright and became the Cross Keys Café and Temperance Hotel, with six bedrooms replacing the old two-table billiard room. Ironically, the building was recently restored to its former glory and became two restaurants – Mississippi's and Huckleberry's – but these closed in January 1996.
(*Tony Smith*)

'Procession of perambulators and proud mothers' read the headline to this photograph in the *Kettering Leader* on Saturday 8 July 1927. During the 1920s and 30s Baby Week was an annual event organised by the Kettering Maternity and Infant Welfare Committee. It always began with a street parade, seen here in Dalkeith Place, followed by tea for mums and their children at the Corn Market Hall. Prams were imaginatively decorated, and prizes and shields were awarded to both adults and their bonny bairns. That evening there would be a garden party and fête at Chesham House in Lower Street, and other events during the week would include film exhibitions and lantern lectures. Kettering Dairy is at the top right of this picture. (*Tony Smith*)

First World War soldiers march along Dalkeith Place in March 1915. Members of the Royal Army Medical Corps and the Army Service Corps were joined by the Scottish Horse returning from a meeting at the Victoria Hall in Gold Street. On the left is Palmers music store, founded by Henry Palmer in Market Street in 1875. The store sold pianos, organs, harmoniums and old violins and offered piano tuning and repairs. It was an agent for His Master's Voice gramophones and records and provided Kettering people with the first popular recorded music and sheet music. Henry's son Tom was a partner for 45 years and died in 1972 aged 83. (*Kettering Civic Society*)

The damage caused in London Road by the worst blizzard this century on 28 March 1916. Buses were halted and rail services were in disarray. By the afternoon, 14 of the 16 telegraph poles in London Road were either down or snapped in two. There were similar scenes in Dryland Street and Rockingham Road, while a chimney smashed through the roof of Charles Speight's house in Bowling Green Road. Local schools closed and there was no phone line to surrounding villages. All telegraph poles were down between Kettering and Wellingborough. It took a full hour for the 8.55am train from Isham to arrive in Kettering, and seven hours for another train to travel the 27 miles from Leicester. (*Tony Smith*)

This was one of many military parades and public gatherings on the Market Place during the early part of the century, when people would be addressed from the former Corn Exchange. This building was converted to a cinema by Leon Vint, and the grand opening was Saturday 16 October 1909, with Arthur Broyden as manager. Admission prices were 2d, 3d and 6d for the stalls, and 9d for the balcony. In 1912 local tradesman and coal merchant John Covington took over, changing the name to The Palace. Five years later it became The Hippodrome under his successor Frank Hawkins, but he went bankrupt in 1922. For many years after closing as a cinema, the building was a popular billiards hall, and now houses shops, a bookmaker and café. Harry Tate and Lillie Langtry were among the many music hall artistes who trod the boards at The Palace. (*Kettering Civic Society*)

Spencer Percival's picture of the annual 'treat' of the Kettering Nonconformist Sunday Schools on 20 July 1915. The massed schools were to unite on the Market Place to sing patriotic hymns after a parade through the town. But so many adults were there that there was no room for the children, and the songs were abandoned. It was the largest Sunday School procession ever seen in the town, despite the weather. Umbrellas proliferate! (*Dick Fairey*)

Members of St Mary's Church, led by Frank Underwood, march up Montagu Street in a Feast Day parade circa 1920. The route continued down Gold Street and along High Street to the parish church for a service. The large building on the left (now Midland Furniture showrooms) was occupied by leather dressers F. S. Bryant for almost half a century. Frederick Sidney Bryant, who founded the firm in Havelock Street, was president of the Poppies Supporters Club for many years. He died in 1959 and his factory closed in 1980. On the corner of Tresham Street is Henry Earl's paper shop (later run for many years by H. G. Brace and Son, newsagents and confectioners). York's had their first TV showrooms on the centre site, now occupied by Christie the bookmaker and Choices video shop. (*Kettering Civic Society*)

Boy scout Kenneth Lawrence, a 12-year-old member of Kettering St Mary's Troop, was presented with a gallantry medal at the Church Institute in Avondale Road in January 1923. The award, for rescuing his little sister from drowning in the Ise Brook, was pinned on him by Sir Arthur de Capell Brooke, vice-chairman of the county council, watched by Mr H. Butlin, J.P., Alderman Charles Wicksteed (with beard), Mr H. W. Bryant (treasurer), Cllr. Thomas Seddon, MBE, and the Rev. F. H. Glaister (vicar of St Mary's). On the extreme right is the sister Kenneth saved with their mother. (*Kettering Civic Society*)

A procession of civic VIPs passes the Royal Hotel en route to the Cenotaph after Kettering was granted the Charter of Incorporation, making it a borough on 29 September 1938. The Lord Lieutenant of Northamptonshire, The Marquess of Exeter, presented the deeds to Charter Mayor John Alfred Gotch at the official ceremony at the Regal cinema (later Granada). Dance music was relayed by loudspeakers to crowds milling outside, and there was a parade of pageantry, with five local brass bands. The *Evening Telegraph* arranged for Gaumont to make a commemorative film which was shown at every cinema in town the following week. Pictured, from left, are mace-bearer Mr A. Price, in a smart green and yellow-braided uniform, the Lord Lieutenant, Charter Mayor, Deputy Charter Mayor Cllr Mrs C. W. Clarke, and the High Sheriff, Major G. R. D. Shaw. (*Kettering Civic Society*)

A crowd gathers outside Kettering Working Men's Club in Wellington Street on 26 August 1921 for the unveiling of a memorial tablet to 33 members killed in the war. The town's oldest and largest club began early in 1887 in disused factory premises in Gas Street (now Meadow Road), belonging to William Neale. That year it bought a plot of land on the new housing estate around Wellington Street to build a new HQ, which had a committee room, games room, bar and concert room. Many ordinary working men became shareholders, paying contributions in weekly instalments. There are six foundation stones dated 5 November 1887, and when the club celebrated its Golden Jubilee in May 1937 its original secretary Frank Sturgess, aged 80, was still in office. The memorial was unveiled by Mr J. J. Dent, president of the National Club and Institute Union, and a laurel wreath was placed above it by Owen Clarke, who lost three brothers. Sadly, the WMC closed in July 1991 through lack of cash after more than 100 years, and the premises were taken over by Kettering Sports and Leisure Club. (*Dick Fairey*)

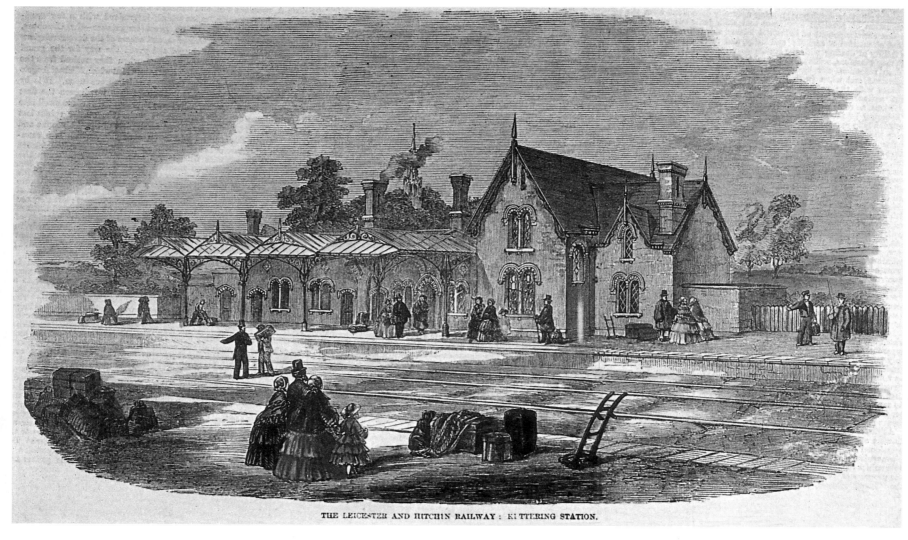

THE LEICESTER AND HITCHIN RAILWAY: KETTERING STATION.

This drawing of Kettering station appeared in the *London Illustrated News* when the line was opened by Midland Railways in 1857. Kettering's population then was only 5,500, but was soon boosted by the prosperity brought by the railway. A seat on the first excursion to Leicester on 7 May cost a shilling, and the first train of 33 carriages carried 300 excited passengers. Large numbers gathered that afternoon for its return. A public holiday was declared for the 'official' opening, and shops and businesses closed so that everyone could celebrate. Some hundreds of Kettering people went in three trains to Bedford, Southill Park and Hitchin. In the evening there were street parties, a concert at the Corn Exchange, and a dinner for 80 VIPs at the Royal Hotel. A new station was built in 1898 and many still mourn the closure of the Cambridge line in 1959 after 93 years. (*Kettering Civic Society*)

An empty station yard during the 1926 General Strike. The national protest against the Government's wage control policy began on May Day, and Kettering people first heard about it on the wireless at 11.30pm the night before. Rail services were chaotic, and within three days most factories in the town were idle. Although the strike passed peacefully in Kettering, a dozen policemen and special constables were on special duty on the platforms at the railway station. Businesses had to collect their own parcels from the Post Office, and even the parish church clock stopped at the end of the week, by which time 2,000 local people were out of work. The strike proved disastrous for the boot and shoe trade, and the TUC called it off on 12 May. (*Dick Fairey*)

This postcard shows 39 clothing workers for Wallis and Linnell who saw action in World War I, most of them in the Northamptonshire Regiment. When this was published, two men had been killed and two were missing in action. Draper Frederic Wallis (1833-1886) began a clothing factory in School Lane in 1856 and the next year teamed up with partner John Linnell. The firm grew to become one of the largest local companies, with factories in School Lane (now Weavers Medical Centre), Regent Street, Woodford, Cottingham, Burton Latimer, Rothwell, Gretton and Brigstock. The business closed in 1979, having exported to 20 countries, employed many hundreds of local people, and made 100,000 service garments during World War II. (*Tony Smith*)

Sixteen police constables lead a solemn procession along Market Place to the Cenotaph on Armistice Day on Sunday 8 November 1925. Dr Tollputt, J.P., on behalf of the town, placed the first laurel wreath at the ceremony. Church bells and factory hooters signalled the start of the two minutes' silence, causing some confusion to motorists at the top of Gold Street. A crowd of 2,000 people heard a brief Armistice Day programme broadcast from Whitehall via a loudspeaker from a bedroom window of the Royal Hotel. Church ministers, massed bands, the St John Ambulance Brigade, scouts, guides and council representatives had set off from Dalkeith Place on a route which included Silver Street, Gold Street and High Street. (*Kettering Civic Society*)

For the first two years after World War I, many hundreds of townspeople joined the Armistice Day service at a temporary wooden cenotaph erected outside the public library opposite the George Hotel stable block. In 1920 wreaths were laid by ex-servicemen, along with ambulance workers and scouts, preceding a drumhead service in the nearby Manor House Field.
(*Kettering Civic Society*)

The Cenotaph ceremony was conducted by the Rev. F. J. Burt, former chaplain and vicar of St Andrew's Church. The uniformed men were inspected by the Lord Lieutenant of the county, Earl Spencer, who also addressed the massed gathering. Many Kettering people brought along their own flowers as a tribute to the 805 Kettering men who gave their lives in the Great War. (*Kettering Civic Society*)

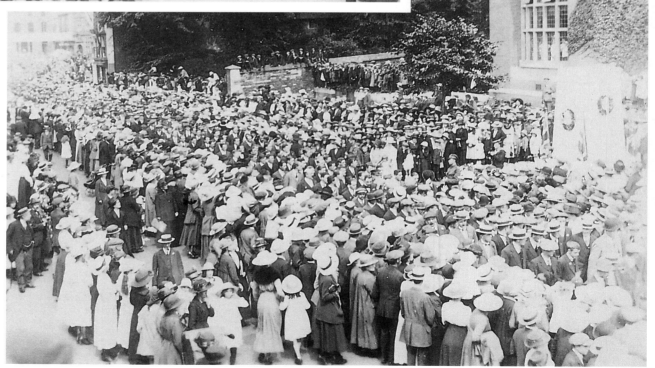

Kettering Armistice Day in November 1921 began with a procession which included this delegation from the urban council. Town clerk John Bond is the man with the wreath, joined by Councillors E. C. Gravestock, H. W. Perkins, H. Coe, L. Richards and town surveyor Mr T. Reader-Smith. A two-minute silence was observed at factories, shops, homes and at the Cenotaph. (*Tony Smith*)

Seldom had Kettering seen such a multitude of people. They had gathered to witness the unveiling of the town's permanent war memorial on Saturday 17 December 1921. The 14 ft. 6 in. Cenotaph, inset, outside the art gallery was designed by Gotch and Saunders and built by local stonemasons W. T. Cox and Co. The people pictured in Sheep Street listened to the service outside because only those with special tickets were allowed in the Manor House gardens. Earlier there was a procession from Market Hill by the British Legion, Northamptonshire Yeomanry, the Scottish Horse Regiment, St John Ambulance Brigade and Kettering Rifle Band. (*Tony Smith* and inset *Robert Wharton*)

Just a section of the crowd which stood in silence for two minutes after the official unveiling of the Cenotaph by the Lord Chamberlain, the Duke of Atholl, in grateful memory of the 805 local men who lost their lives in the Great War. The Duke gave an eloquent and moving address after inspecting the Kettering Company of the 4th Battalion Northamptonshire Regiment, the Territorial Guard of Honour, and his Scottish Horse comrades. The memorial was blessed by the Bishop of Peterborough, flanked by the Rev. C. B. Lucas (Kettering rector and chaplain), the Rev. F. H. Glaister (vicar of St Mary's Church), in ceremonial robes. Then 'Rock of Ages' was sung, accompanied by the Rifle Band. The Bishop later dedicated the new parish church clock and bells and unveiled a memorial cross in the churchyard. (*Dick Fairey*)

The Rev. W. M. Fuller, grandson of Andrew Fuller, was chosen to lay the foundation stone of the Sunday School Assembly Rooms next to Fuller Baptist Church in Gold Street on 19 May 1879, at the time the Rev. J. B. Mayers was pastor. It was here that youngsters used to marvel at the first Victorian magic lantern shows on Sunday evenings. In 1931 the lower front of this block was converted into shops to bring in extra revenue for the church. For many years classes at Kettering Eisteddfod were judged in the Assembly Rooms, which were demolished in 1977 to make way for the new Boots store in the Newborough Centre (now Newlands). They were replaced by new premises at the rear of the chapel. (*Fuller Church*)

Snooker legend Joe Davis won the eighth of his record 15 world titles when the championship final was staged at the former Co-op Central Hall in Montagu Street on 5 and 6 April 1934. The early frames between title holder Davis and Tom Newman had been played at Nottingham, with Davis leading 16-14. The final two days at Kettering saw the champion clinch the match 25-22 to win the now-famous silver trophy lifted most recently by Stephen Hendry. Both finalists stayed at the Royal Hotel, and on the first morning were shown around the *Evening Telegraph* offices then in Dryland Street. The historic handover of the trophy was made by Kettering Urban Council chairman Cllr H. Hodge. Also in the picture, from the left, are promoter Howarth Nuttall, Tom Newman, Evan Marlow, Kettering snooker champion Jack Old, marker Willie Leigh and Central Hall manager Bert Toseland. Davis returned to Kettering in October 1942 for a week of exhibition matches to raise money for the town's Immediate Aid Fund. (*Brian Old*)

Chief Scout Lord Arthur Somers-Cocks (1887-1944) is greeted by local boy scouts and girl guides outside Kettering station on his visit during World War II. The former Governor of Victoria, Australia, took an active part in the scout movement from 1920 to the end of his life. In 1932 he became a Chief Commissioner to Lord Baden-Powell, who nominated him acting Chief Scout during his tour of South Africa in 1935. He was made deputy the following year and was designated by the founder to succeed him in January 1941. He died in July 1944 after a serious illness. An American airman can be seen with his truck in the background of this photograph. (*Reg Abbott*)

Spencer Percival's historic picture of the first wireless installed at the old workhouse (now St Mary's Hospital) and presented by Frank Butlin in March 1925. Among those pictured are Mr Hutchinson (chairman of the Board of Guardians), Mr Matthew Wilson (vice-chairman), the Rev. F. Dean, Miss Lammie, Mrs Chamberlain and members of the Butlin family, who donated the radio in memory of their father, the late Mr J. T. Butlin of Rothwell, a member of the Board of Guardians for 28 years. They listened to a Birmingham concert by the Station Wind Quartet, and live music at teatime from the Trocadero in London, and the old lady engrossed in the broadcast was 94 years old. (*Tony Smith*)

In the early days of radio, Alfred Freeman had a stall on Kettering market where the public could listen in on several sets of earphones. His aerial was suspended between a street lamp and a shop, and such demonstrations were in aid of hospital funds. The Kettering Radio and Physical Society met at the Victoria Picture Palace Café in Gold Street during the 1930s and held exhibitions at the Central Hall in Montagu Street. This picture was taken in February 1923. (*Kettering Civic Society*)

A horsedrawn float, covered in flowers and loaded with children, waits outside the Wesleyan Church in Silver Street to join a Temperance procession through the town in 1906. On the left is Ruby Cottage, built in Ebenezer Place by watchmaker Mr Wheeler (see page 12). It was also the childhood home of bill-poster Fred Bye (see page 134).
(*Tony Smith*)

Those of you who bought my first book, *Kettering Revisited*, will have seen two pictures on page 156 of a Temperance procession in 1906, one approaching the top of Gold Street and the other taken almost from this very spot in High Street near Bakehouse Hill. The only difference between the two photographs is the shop on the corner of Crispin Place (now Lewin's), one featuring F. Smith and Sons and this one showing The Grotto (see page 130), pictured a decade later.
(*John Darker*)

Here's a people-packed picture by Spencer Percival of the annual Feast Sunday parade marching along Dalkeith Place on 4 July 1926. At the Carrington Street junction, a motor car pauses to allow a horse and trap to go by. Among those taking part in the long procession were police, firemen, ambulance brigade, cadets, scouts and Territorials, with seemingly the entire population of Kettering behind them! Wallace and English proudly display their greetings cards and postcards in their window, and top right is the Parish Church School in Horsemarket. (*Tony Smith*)

The Kettering St John Ambulance Corps weekend camp at Great Oakley in 1925. District Superintendent Adnitt of Northampton is seen 'listening in' to wireless concerts from London on this first occasion ever that the ambulance corps had been equipped with radio. The St John Ambulance Brigade in Kettering had 10 divisions numbering 200 men at this time, including members from Corby, Geddington and the Midland Railway. It also had three nursing divisions with 80 nursing sisters, detachments at Corby, Rothwell and Geddington and 50 girl cadets.
(*Kettering Civic Society*)

The coffin of Sir Alfred East leaves the art gallery which bears his name for his funeral on Saturday 4 October 1913. More than 7,500 people paid their respects when his body lay in state for three days, and hundreds more joined the procession to the Parish Church led by Lady East and family, before his burial at Kettering cemetery. Sir Alfred (pictured) was born on 15 December 1844 in Lower Street and was a pupil of Kettering Grammar School. He studied art at Glasgow and Paris and was described as England's greatest living landscape artist. The art gallery, designed by J. A. Gotch, was built to house his paintings. It was opened by Earl Spencer on 31 July 1913, but Sir Alfred was too ill to attend and he died on 28 September that year. (*Kettering Civic Society*)

# 6. Shops

The old Grotto sweet shop on the corner of High Street and Crispin Place will revive many childhood memories. Upstairs was a little café serving tea and cakes. The building has been Lewin's cooked meat shop since 1961. Ted Lewin, who died in 1993, bought it in 1940 when his own shop in High Street (later Sketchleys) was threatened with demolition. When this did not happen, he rented out The Grotto and did not take it over for another 21 years. Ted's father Ernest founded the family firm with a shop in Newland Street (now the Button Boutique) in 1922, and at one time also had premises in Montagu Street. The Crispin Place shop is now run by the founder's grandson Bill, who has worked there since 1966.
(*Kettering Civic Society*)

## Wells Grocery

Wells, Kettering's oldest grocery and bakery shop, pictured in Walkers Lane, off High Street, in 1936, when it sold loaves for 2$^1$/2d and would fill a 2 lb jam jar with treacle! The tiny shop, with its small Georgian window panes, was taken over by Joseph Wells in 1851 and handed down to his son Alfred when he died in 1899. After Alfred died in 1912, his son James ran it for 24 years. The shop baked bread at the rear of the premises and made home deliveries in a horse-drawn van. On the right was Woolworths, which sold sweets for 2d and 4d a quarter in the 1930s, and spectacles at 6d for the lenses and 6d for the frames. On the left used to be F. Spence and Sons, furnishers and cabinet makers, founded in 1862, whose premises were demolished in 1932 to make way for Marks and Spencer. (*Kettering Civic Society*)

## Hall's Corner

Ernest Albert Hall owned a thriving drapers and milliners business in Market Street in the first quarter of the century, claiming the best dresses and hats in town. In the early 1900s gas lamps were even hung in front of the windows so that goods on sale were visible at night. The shop on this page has been demolished and is now the Yorkshire Bank. The Golden Lion became the Gaiety, then Watercress Harry's, and now Manny's. Shoe firm Timpsons had a shop, office and factory behind Hall's before building a new factory in Bath Road in 1922, demolished in 1996 for housing.
(*Kettering Civic Society*)

By the 1920s Mr Hall was running three shops in Market Street, No. 6 (opposite page) and Nos. 25 and 26 across the road (left). No. 25, built in 1895, later became Lillyman and Corvesor's first ironmongers (see page 140) and is now The Private Shop, Kettering's first sex shop, opened in the 1970s.
(*Kettering Civic Society*)

Although none of the three Halls shops in Market Street were on a corner, they were called Hall's Corner after a previous store in High Street, Desborough (pictured right).
(*Kettering Civic Society*)

133

James Nichols, the rope and twine merchants at the top of Market Hill, circa 1911. The first floor was occupied by Rockley's, Kettering's only bill-posters, managed by the shipping merchant Edward Bye. His son Obed, known as 'Fred', joined his father in 1924 and was a bill-poster for 49 years, taking over the business when his father retired. Fred, who lived in Ruby Cottage in Ebenezer Place before moving to Mill Road, turned 89 in August 1996. (*Kettering Civic Society*)

The ever-busy fish and poultry shop run by B. H. Miles and Co. next to the Newland Street passage during the 1920s. Hanging outside, exposed to the elements, are the day's prize fowl (what would public health inspectors make of this today?). Also on offer are fillets of bloater, cod, haddock, plaice and halibut. The shop closed during the depression of the 1930s. (*Kettering Civic Society*)

A Thornycroft lorry delivering provisions to Lipton's grocers and tea merchants store at the top of Gold Street during the 1926 general strike. The store was a popular feature of Gold Street for decades, and it prided itself on its personal service. Customers' change would be returned via a container propelled along overhead wires from the cash desk. (*Kettering Civic Society*)

## Chalkley's

Chalkley's family-run clothing store closed in February 1996 after almost 90 years in the town. Founder Arthur Chalkley is pictured with his assistant Mrs Bridgeford outside his first shop on the corner of King Street and Wellington Street in 1920. Mr Chalkley started out selling drapery from a handcart in 1907. At the height of their success, Chalkley's had eight stores in Kettering. (*Brian Hughes*)

One of the two Chalkley's stores in Silver Street with a prospective customer of years to come waiting outside. This shop later became the Army Careers Office and is now empty. The last remaining shop was based in Silver Street from 1923 and was previously the Midland Railway parcels office (see page 34). The shop was famous for its corsets, and kitted out generations of local schoolchildren in uniforms. (*Brian Hughes*)

Bird's wholesale fruit shop in Montagu Street was one of Kettering's oldest and much-loved family concerns. It was opened at the turn of the century by George Henry Bird, who would travel to London twice a week to buy produce from Covent Garden and The City Sale Rooms, which was later sent to Kettering by train. On his death in 1943 the business was taken over by his nephew, also George, and his brother Stan. It later moved to premises in Carrington Street (next to the Angel Hotel) and was sold in May 1984 to M. and H. Produce. Stan Bird, who worked for his uncle when he was 16, was a well-known figure in the town and was president of Kettering Chamber of Trade and Commerce in 1965.
(*Kettering Civic Society*)

Kettering's most famous 'one-man' business was Jack Cross's newsagents, which closed in 1974 after 68 years in the town. Jack Cross sen. was originally a clicker who sold papers from his Wellington Street home as a sideline. He is pictured outside his first shop – 300-year-old thatched premises in Northall Street, which included Alf Gutteridge's barber shop. The cottage roof had to be hosed down during a fierce fire at the nearby Mobbs shoe factory in 1924. Jack was the first wholesaler in Kettering and, at one time, printed his own 'slip' editions of the *Daily Mail*, inserting late news about Test Matches (pictured) and election results into each paper when they arrived from London at 3.30am! He also used to run 'Dot's Selections', a daily list of racing tips he would sell for sixpence a time. Jack died in 1951 at the age of 66. (*Jack Cross*)

## Jack Cross

Jack's son, Jack Cross Jr. became involved in the business when it moved to premises near the top of Northall Street (now Sainsbury's) in 1930. A Corby branch was opened in 1934, and in 1947 Jack Jr. took over the Central Printing Works behind the shop. The Kettering shop's frontage was filled by shutters, and when these were pulled up in summer the front was entirely open – no windows between customers and goods on sale. Cross vans would deliver to all local newsagents and many surrounding villages. (*Jack Cross*)

Between 1951 and 1974 business expanded tenfold. In 1968 Jack had a new warehouse and printing works built. By then the shop was open 12 hours a day and people used to say, 'If you can't get what you want from Jack Cross you won't get it anywhere.' Jack was forced to retire when his shop was demolished by the council for the town's inner ring road and he sold the printing works to Surridge Dawson. He is now a sprightly 82 years old and the famous shop shutters form the doors of his garage at his home in Masefield Road. (*Jack Cross*)

It was the end of an era when Dalkeith Ironmongers closed their Horsemarket shop in September 1992. The firm was founded in 1936 by Frank Corvesor and Ernest Lillyman, former trainees with Bell and Billows on Bakehouse Hill. Their first shop (above left) was 25 Market Street (now Kettering's sex shop!) but they soon took over the shop next door as well (below left). After World War II they moved to a single shop in Horsemarket (above right) and in 1946 acquired larger premises along the road on the corner of Carrington Street (below right). In 1981 the firm was handed down to the partners' sons, Leo Corvesor and Richard Lillyman, but sadly the recession and competition from DIY superstores forced them to quit in 1992. The nineteenth century farmyard and stables, used to store barbed wire and netting behind the store, disappeared when the premises were taken over by a cycle shop. (*Frank Corvesor*)

# 7. People

Benjamin Blackwell Percival was born in British School Lane (now Dalkeith Avenue) in 1840. He was an auctioneer at Kettering Cattle Market before becoming an antiques dealer and picture restorer trading from his Old Curiosity Shop just above the Temperance Hall in Gold Street. He was immortalised in a W. B. Gash oil painting 'The Connoisseur', presented to the town in 1905 after showing at the Royal Academy. There is a display of Benny working in his shop in the Manor House Museum. This picture was taken by his son Spencer, the local press photographer who also published picture postcards. Many more of his photographs can be seen elsewhere in this book. (*Kettering Civic Society*)

Midland Railway staff pictured next to the goods yard at the bottom of Station Road before World War I. In those halcyon days, steam trains were the cheapest and swiftest way to travel. The station was always busy (unlike now!) with a large workforce of porters, ticket collectors, clerks and officials, not to mention the refreshment rooms and W. H. Smith's lending library. From the goods yard, wonderful dray horses would deliver coal and other essential items. At one time Station Road was cobbled, enabling an easier journey for the shire horses. (*Dick Fairey*)

In the early 1900s a group of workers take a break posing by their barrow of ladders. The cart belongs to the Kettering Window Cleaning Company, which also offered to beat and re-lay carpets! Does anyone recognise the street? (*Kettering Civic Society*)

Who knows what these old-timers were talking about when they lit their pipes on the upper floor of the pavilion at Wicksteed Park? Like thousands of others, they were enjoying a day trip to the biggest leisure park in the Midlands when this 'striking' picture was taken in 1927. (*Dick Fairey*)

Now you see them – now you don't! It's hats off to these members of Kettering's Salvation Army Band outside the corps' citadel in Regent Street during the 1920s. Which of these two pictures was taken first (or why) is not clear. Maybe it had started to rain – certainly the men do not appear to have moved a muscle, hats or no hats. The lady in the middle of the front row obviously decided it would be too complicated to remove her bonnet! (*Robert Wharton*)

The Salvation Army Band is believed to have formed in the 1880s, and it was very popular at open-air services. In 1917 Albert Munn became bandmaster and did not retire until 1956. He recruited many newcomers from outside as the band became widely regarded as one of the country's best. It kept going in World War II and even made a broadcast for BBC radio. The Kettering corps' morning service was broadcast live on Radio 4 many years later, in August 1987.
(*Tony Smith*)

The switchboard ladies of Kettering Telephone Exchange in Ebenezer Place on 6 September 1927. From left, they are Margaret and Marjorie Wardle, Florrie Baker, Miss Bailey, Winnie West and Nora Pitts. Mr Kerr, a linesman from Wellingborough, is on the far right. The exchange had moved there from Church Walk in 1903 and remained in Ebenezer Place until moving to the Newcastle building above the main Post Office in Lower Street in 1937. It moved again to a seven-storey building in Trafalgar Road in 1979 at a cost of £5 million. The exchange closed on 24 March 1995.
(*Winnie Bailey*)

George Harrison (with apron and moustache) and his assistant Will Rowlatt pose with customers outside his Gold Street barber shop in 1911. George (1876-1950) became famous for his sketches and poems of the Northamptonshire countryside. Born in Workhouse Lane (now Dryland Street), he went to the British School in School Lane (now the Four Seasons Day Centre). He studied art in Antwerp with his mentor, W. B. Gash. His drawings, poems, and articles appeared in the *Kettering Leader* from the 1920s to the 40s. George also had a barber shop in Rockingham Road (now the Raj Indian Restaurant). This picture was loaned by Pam Dyson, daughter of Mr Rowlatt, who later ran a hairdressing business from his home in King Street, Kettering. (*Pam Dyson*)

The cast of the operetta *Cinderella: The Enchanted Rose*, performed by pupils of Park Road Junior School in November 1906. The school in Wood Street opened in 1898 with John Glover Anderson as its first headmaster, with 147 girls and 146 boys. For two years before it was built, classes were held at nearby Carey Baptist Church hall under Miss Mary Jane Owen. One of the most influential heads in its history was Les Smith (1954-74) but the best remembered teacher was the formidable Miss Gladys Riseley, MBE (inset), Kettering's 'Miss Music', who taught there for 40 years until she retired as deputy head in 1970. Pictured here (left to right) are: back row, Mabel Spriggs, Hilda Morris, Hilda Sturgess, Ellen Abbott, Dora Berry, Hilda Risdill, Grace Neale; second row, Grace Shatford, Bert Hudson, Daisy Payne, Wilfred Lilley, Charlie Boss, Elsie Wright, Fred Winston, Jessie Chater, Fred Dixon, Elsie Middleton; sitting, Mary Burton, Cyril Nunneley, Connie Middleton, Alice Shipton, Hilda Essam; seated on floor, unknown except William Nursey (pixie on far right). The word 'road' was dropped from the school's title in 1970.
(*Park Junior School*)

## The Rev. J.M. Watson

The Reverend J.M. Watson, pastor of the Toller Church in Gold Street for 17 years, was an inspiring religious leader in the Victorian era. He trained for the priesthood in his native Belfast, labouring in a local Wesleyan ministry from 1859 to 1867. He came to Kettering to take over from the Reverend Hinchcliffe Higgins in January 1879. He was instrumental in the erection of the Sunday School buildings in Meeting Lane for £3,400. The church membership had more than doubled by the time he resigned in 1895. Twice married, the Reverend Watson went to a church in Morecambe in 1900 until he retired in 1909.
(*Kettering Civic Society*)

My late father, Rodger Smith, was troop leader of the 10th Fuller Scouts, seated second from right in the front row of this 1947 picture taken in the Fuller Institute gymnasium in Gold Street. Next to him, guarding the much-prized Butlin Shield, is scout master Bill Draper. Among the other scouts are Geoff Ralph, Arthur Payne, Peter Taylor, Alec Austin, Fred Jellis, Wilf Capps, Ken Timms, Jack Ridout, Ray Mabbutt and Jack Prestidge. My dad, who worked at the Central Garage and later as an agent for Pearl Assurance, died from a coronary thrombosis in 1968 at the age of 44.

(*Tony Smith*)

## Watercress Harry

Harry Wood, better known as Watercress Harry, was a colourful character who roamed the Kettering area at the turn of the century. He came from Leicester, where he had been a well-known boxer. He eked out a living selling watercress, picked from spots only he knew for miles around. Children loved him and would rush out into the street when they saw him with his basket. Although resembling a tramp with his dirty coat and bowler hat, he was a real gentleman and was always polite. Sometimes local housewives would take pity on him and save him some Sunday dinner. He slept rough, occasionally seeking shelter in the workhouse, and spent most of his pennies on beer. In the winter months he would sell oranges from a hessian sack to local farms. He died in 1912, but his memory was honoured when the former Gaiety pub in Market Street was named after him. It is now known as Manny's after the landlord – another former boxer! (*Robert Wharton*)

Despite dull weather, more than 600 people turned out when Kettering hosted the regional Fire Brigade Union's annual competitions for the first time on Saturday 22 August 1908. There were teams from Northamptonshire, Cambridge, Huntingdon, Lincolnshire, Leicestershire, Bedfordshire and Nottinghamshire, and the Kettering brigade was led by Captain Riddle and Second Officer Dixon. The day began with the annual meeting of local union members at the Royal Hotel, and at noon a procession started from Market Hill and proceeded along Rockingham Road (as pictured here) to the Poppies football ground. It was led by the town band, followed by the Kettering No. 1 steamer, carrying the three cups to be won at the competitions (horse-cart, steamer, and six-man manual contests). Among those taking part were firemen from the Kettering Co-op Society, but no local teams were among the overall winners. (*Robert Wharton*)

Captain Brewer and his crew outside the old Kettering Fire Station in Market Street circa 1930. The £1,530 building, opened on 22 October 1926, included a hose-drying and drill tower, recreation room, fully-equipped workshop and bathroom. One engine, bought in 1917 for £900, was previously housed at Robinson's garage in Montagu Street while the other was in the playground of the Boys National School in Horsemarket. The building later became the town's ambulance station and is now the Oasis Centre and Citizen's Advice Bureau. Pictured (back row) W. Frisby, H. Chapman, B. Willis, A. Plowman, W. Proctor, R. Tompkins, B. Lovell; (front row) H. Farmer, H. Taylor, A. V. Innes, Captain M. Brewer (Chief Officer), G. Dennet, E. Knight, H. Gould. (*Kettering Fire Station*)

Pictured on the old Cattle Market are the heroes who tackled the disastrous fire at Mobbs and Lewis' last factory in Carrington Street on 17 August 1921. The brave men battled to put it out despite dense smoke and falling timber and machinery. The brigade, led by Captain Brewer (centre), prevented flames spreading from the old two-storey section to the three-storey building and the neighbouring Thompson and Sons shoe factory. Both the steam and motor engines were used to pump water from a tank at the top of Dryland Street, while a crowd of onlookers were kept back by the police. Flames were first spotted by a passer-by shortly after the 140 workers had left the factory at 5pm. Many thousands of pounds worth of damage was caused to the building and lathes. The photograph was taken by Charles Speight (see page 72).

(*Kettering Fire Station*)

## John Alfred Gotch

Charles Speight's portrait of John Alfred Gotch in his robes as Charter Mayor when Kettering became a borough in 1938. Mr Gotch was from a distinguished family which first came to Kettering over 250 years ago. Their influence transformed the town, providing three generations of civic leadership and introducing the shoe trade in the eighteenth century. J. A. Gotch was Kettering's first resident practising architect and, with his partner Charles Saunders, designed the most striking buildings in the town, including the old Post Office block, the art gallery, Liberal Club, St Mary's Church, many Kettering schools, and other premises featured in this book. Mr Gotch was chairman of Kettering and District Art Society, chairman of Kettering magistrates, and a Justice of the Peace for almost 50 years. The former Kettering Grammar School pupil died in January 1942, aged 89. (*Tony Smith*)

A street entertainer with his barrel organ and monkey outside the Westminster Bank in Market Street in 1922. This was quite a common sight in Kettering in the first quarter of the century. Readers may remember another picture of such a barrel organ being played in Rockingham Road on page 104 of *Kettering Revisited.* (*Dick Fairey*)

A Spencer Percival picture of a 'pretty ankle' parade, which was a popular feature of shoe factory garden parties and fetes in the 1920s. The arbitrators, of course, were the most careful judges! (*Dick Fairey*)

## Charles Wicksteed

The unmistakeable features of Charles Wicksteed, a great humanitarian and benefactor with a remarkable record of public service to his adoptive town of Kettering. Born in Leeds in 1847, this seventh son of a Unitarian minister came to the town in 1871 and five years later set up his own hugely successful engineering works in Digby Street. He soon became a respected townsman and staunch Liberal. He took an active role in public affairs, serving for many years on Kettering Urban Council and as an Alderman on the county council. But, of course, he is best remembered for founding Wicksteed Park, a unique children's playground, which in 1996 celebrated its 75th anniversary. Incredibly, he was himself 74 when the park opened and he died in March 1931, just a few days before his 84th birthday. He is pictured above in his car in the 1920s with his constant companion, his dog Jerry, in whose memory a statue was erected in the gardens of Wicksteed Park. (*Robert Wicksteed and Kettering Civic Society*)

# 8. Wicksteed Park

An early picture postcard of Wicksteed Park, which in 1996 celebrated its 75th anniversary with a host of events and special offers. Since 1921 when the lake and grounds were opened to the public, the park has been administered by a charity trust set up by founder Charles Wicksteed (see previous page). This visionary engineer provided the town (and visitors) with a much-needed amenity when there was precious little to occupy the leisure time of the working man. When it was created, 'Wickies' was the first children's pleasure park of its kind in the country. (*Robert Wharton*)

157

In 1911 Charles Wicksteed bought pastureland near Barton Seagrave with the original idea of developing a model village of more than 150 low-cost pre-fab houses with decent gardens, surrounding a large grass area and lake. But after World War I, the lifting of building restrictions and the creation of the first housing estates made his plans redundant and he went ahead with a recreational park. Preliminary digging and levelling was carried out including the uprooting of 3,000 trees. The 30-acre boating lake, pictured, was constructed after World War I on the site of the original stream which still provides its water supply.
(*Robert Wharton and Kettering Civic Society*)

Early slides were a far cry from the modern metal version with all its safety features. The first primitive swings were put up with larch poles, tied together at the top with chains, for a Sunday School 'Treat' at the park. These playthings, which were not taken down, were so successful that Charles Wicksteed set to work designing new equipment at his engineering factory, which were eventually sold to countries all over the world.
(*Tony Smith*)

These youngsters could not resist the lure of the lake during the 1930s, so they rolled up their trousers and skirts for a paddle. Initially Mr Wicksteed provided a small number of rowing boats, but by the 1960s the fleet numbered more than 100. In its early days people were apt to fall into the shallow lake. Apparently up to a dozen took an involuntary ducking each Bank Holiday. The park, therefore, kept spare clothing for those who fell in, which they wore as their own togs dried! (*Kettering Civic Society*)

During the 1920s Charles Wicksteed built a two-acre playground with 70 free amusements. They had such fancy names as the Giant Stride (a kind of Maypole with swinging ropes), the Plank Swing or Jazz (a cross between a swing and a see-saw), and Trapeze Rings (seven ropes dangling from a larch pole). By the 1930s attractions included merry-go-rounds, joy wheels, parallel bars, whirling platforms (pictured here), horizontal ladders, rocking horses, and the popular sand pit. Many of these survived until 1988 when there was a drastic £250,000 revamp of the playground, introducing the latest brightly-coloured play equipment. (*Robert Wharton*)

A super aerial shot of Wicksteed Park during the late 1930s – there is another, including the lake, at the back of this book. Here you can see the pavilion and rose gardens, children's playground, and a few dozen black cars with picnickers. The picture includes the miniature railway station, and on the other side of the A6 are open fields on which Kettering Grammar School and St Edwards Primary School were later built. On the left there are tennis courts and a putting green. (*Kettering Civic Society*)

Wicksteed Park was not just a recreation ground for the people of Kettering. Special trains, buses, and charabancs brought a million summer visitors by the 1930s. By now the park could boast a running and cycle track, a paddle boating pool, an aviary with many species of birds, and a monkey house. During the 1930s the park also began making its own ice cream, which has since won many national awards. (*Tony Smith*)

These fun miniature cars soon became established favourites with younger visitors in the 1950s. Other new attractions during this period included a nine-and-a-half acre golf course, a 37 ft helter-skelter and a Pets Corner which featured llamas, deer and monkeys stocked by Wellingborough Zoo. (*Tony Smith*)

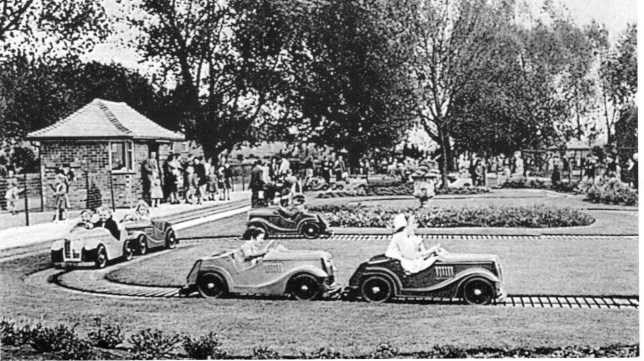

Since the day it opened in 1931, pictured here, the lakeside miniature railway has been the park's most popular family ride. Incredibly its two original engines, King Arthur (seen here) and the Lady of the Lake are still running. The original railway, which ran for one-and-a-half miles, was built by a Staffordshire firm for around £3,000, including £410 for each engine. (*Tony Smith*)

All aboard! Passengers in their open-top carriages wave to the camera. The two 'old faithfuls' were to be joined by the Western-style Cheyenne train at the Wicksteed Village Trust's Golden Jubilee in 1956. At the railway's 50th anniversary in April 1981, the first ever passenger, Robert Wicksteed, took over the driving seat. The railway still carries more than 200,000 passengers a year. (*Tony Smith*)

The growing number of cars in the 1950s meant the population was able to travel greater distances to get to the park, which sometimes caused a problem when they all arrived as shown in this picture, taken from the roof of the pavilion. In 1956 parking rules had to be introduced to cope with the traffic flow, and that year a golf course provided extra parking space for 2,000 vehicles. In the 1960s police and the AA set up diversions on peak days to ease the snarl-up in London Road. The town's longest traffic jam came when 60,000 children and their parents flocked to the Tingha and Tucker Club annual meeting in August 1965. At one point the queue stretched back through Kettering and almost to Broughton!

(*Tony Smith*)

# 9. Anniversaries

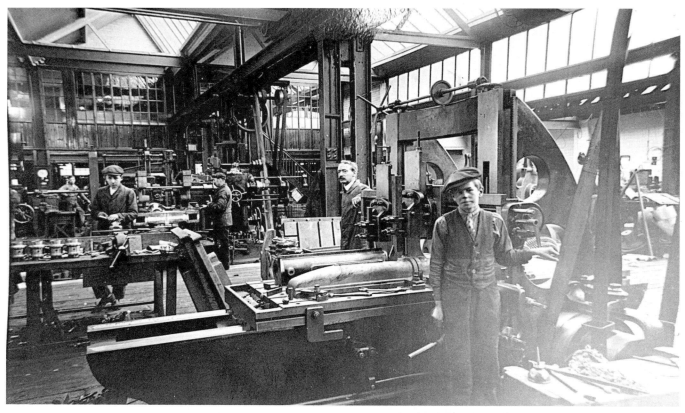

The Timson Perfecta workshop in Bath Road during the early 1920s. The family firm, which celebrated its centenary in June 1996, was founded in the cellar of a house in Victoria Street by engineer Arthur Richardson Timson. Later he began making bicycles in a garden shed in St Peter's Avenue and in the early 1900s, the company – then known as Timson, Bullock and Barber – turned out an early motorised bicycle delightfully called the Ketterina (also pictured), which Mr Timson himself rode between 1908 and 1910. The firm pioneered the first rotary press for the paper and printing trade in 1907. It was the start of an export business that was to take the world by storm. From its new works in Catesby Street and Bath Road, printing presses were shipped to Europe, Australia, North and South America, India, Africa and the Far East. (*Timsons*)

Two rotary presses (below) on delivery lorries pictured outside the Catesby Street premises, established in 1903 after a spell in Montagu Street (now Newmans ironmongers). Arthur's son, Ernest, pictured, took over as managing director in 1940, a post he held until he retired in 1978. He carried on as chairman until he died, aged 85, in 1987. In 1954, the year Arthur died, Timsons acquired the former Primitive Methodist Church in Bath Road, which is still used for storage (see *Kettering Revisited*, page 133). Arthur was awarded the MBE and Ernest the OBE. The firm still has family connections – the founder's granddaughter Jane is a director. (*Timsons*)

Children play games on the lawn outside St Peter's School in Headlands shortly after it opened on 7 May 1946. The mixed preparatory school, which in 1996 celebrated its Golden Jubilee, is based at Sunnylands, a neo-Jacobean house designed by J. A. Gotch for shoe firm giant William Timpson, founder of the footwear factory and its chain of shops. The school began with 50 children and three staff compared to today's roll call of 175 children, 29 teachers and 13 domestic staff. The Victorian building has four acres of grounds and the school has had only four headteachers in half a century. (*St Peter's School*)

Miss Diana Laidler, one of the original teachers at St Peter's School in 1946, supervises school meals. A Kindergarten block was added in 1949 and the nursery takes pre-school children from the age of three. An upper school for senior girls only (11 to 16 years) was established at nearby Angus House in 1953. Famous former pupils include Lord Damian and Lady Charlotte Anne, children of the Duke and Duchess of Buccleuch, who attended during the 1970s. (*St Peter's School*)

Boys do their exercises in the main hall of Hawthorn Road School, which celebrated its centenary in 1994. It was built for the Kettering School Board by George Valentine Henson to designs by Gotch and Saunders at a cost of £2,800. Initially there were three infant classes with 94 pupils, under headmistress Miss Clark and her assistant Miss Brookes. A junior school with six more classrooms, each accommodating between 32 and 60 children, was built by Mr O. P. Drever in 1905 for £3,717, with Mr W. H. Cartwright as head. This picture was taken in 1911. The clerestory windows are still there, but the parquet floor and wooden panelling have long gone in favour of a more modern finish. (*Winnie Bailey*)

The school playground remains the same today, although the wall (left) separating boys from the girls has been knocked down. In the early part of the century children stayed on until 11 or 12, and in some cases, 14, if they failed to meet the required standard. Most left to go straight into work. In those days pupils wrote on slates with slate pencils, and while discipline was strict, only boys were caned. This picture, again from 1911, was probably taken on Empire Day, celebrated each year on 24 May, Queen Victoria's birthday. Parents, pupils and staff built a swimming pool in 1964 and three mobile buildings were added in the late 1980s. Some 4,000 children have passed through the school since it opened.
(*Winnie Bailey*)

## Ronald Tree Nursery School

The county's first-ever nursery school celebrated its 60th anniversary in 1994. The Ronald Tree Nursery School, in Laburnum Crescent, was named after the then MP for Market Harborough (inset), who lived at Kelmarsh Hall. He gave £1,000 for the funding of the nursery in the grounds of the new Avondale School. For the first year, running costs were met by voluntary donations and it was taken over by the local Board of Education in April 1935. The first headteacher was Miss Honor Impey (later Butlin) and in its early days children came from as far as Rothwell and Burton Latimer. A cook was also employed to provide breakfast and lunch, after which children rested on canvas camp beds. This picture from the 1930s shows children playing in the sand pit which still exists today. (*Honor Butlin*)

## Rockingham Road Pleasure Park

In 1994 the centenary of Rockingham Road Pleasure Park was celebrated with a procession and unveiling of a plaque. It was officially opened in May 1894 on 10 acres of land between William Street and Weekley Hall Wood. The ceremony was performed by J. T. Stockburn, chairman of the Local Board, after a parade through Kettering which featured the town's famous steam fire engine, the Fuller Mission Band, and a group of cyclists from the Working Men's Club. Work on tennis courts and bowling greens was completed in 1912. During World War I the Scottish Cavalry had its cookhouse in the park. For many years there was a children's paddling pool, which was dismantled in the 1980s and turned into a play area and toy train station. The cast-iron Victorian drinking fountain (right) given by shoemaker John Bryan was vandalised and placed in storage in Westfield Museum in 1972. There it remained for the next decade until a local group, led by hotelier Sylvia McQuade, raised money to restore it and place it in the Horsemarket flower garden. (*Tony Smith*)

A 1950s picture of Fuller Baptist Church, which celebrated its 300th anniversary in 1996. It was named after its famous minister Andrew Fuller, who in 1792 helped found the world's first missionary society (see page 21). The present chapel in Gold Street, seating 1,000 people, was built in 1861 for £3,636 raised by voluntary subscription. The foundation stone was laid by Sir Morton Peto. A small burial ground at the rear includes the graves of the Reverend Fuller (1754 -1815) and shoemaker and banker John Cooper Gotch (1771-1852) whose father Tom first introduced the shoe trade to the district in 1778. (*Fuller Church*)

These splendid whiskered old gentlemen are delegates of the Baptist Missionary Society pictured outside Fuller Church in Gold Street when they celebrated the society's centenary in 1892. The BMS was formed at a meeting of ministers in the parlour of Martha Wallis's home in Lower Street (see page 21). Within a year William Carey (1781-1834) – inset – sailed to India as the first modern missionary, and it took seven years before the first Hindu was baptised in the Christian faith. The former shoemaker stayed in India for 40 years, and became a college professor, translating the Bible into 40 languages, including Sanskrit, thus making him the world's second greatest linguist of all time. (*Fuller Church*)

Kettering Town Harriers celebrated their centenary in 1994. In its early days the club, previously known as the Crispin Harriers and Kettering Cross Keys Harriers, took top honours in cross country championships at county and national level. In 1908 one member, William 'Buff Coates won a bronze medal for England in the Olympic Games, and in 1958 a women's section was formed. Today the club is based at Kettering Leisure Village off Northampton Road. The above photograph shows the Ernest Thomson County Championship Cup winners of 1931. From left, E. Parkinson, E. Denny, D. Dixon, E. Thompson (president), E. Boyfield, T. Reeves and P. Goodman. (*Tony Smith*)